AD Architectural Design Profile
AD/USC LOOK AT LA

Los Angeles

Guest Editor: Derek Walker

LA EDITORIAL TEAM GRAEME MORLAND CHRIS DAWSON PANOS KOULERMOS JOHN NICOLAIS CHARLES CALVO
LONDON EDITORIAL TEAM DEREK WALKER JAN LARRANCE DAVID REDDICK
PHOTOGRAPHIC EDITORS JOHN NICOLAIS JAN LARRANCE DEREK WALKER
LAYOUT DEREK WALKER
AD EDITORIAL STAFF IAN LATHAM PENELOPE FARRANT RICHARD CHEATLE

WELCOME TO

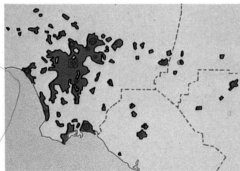

LAX Christmas

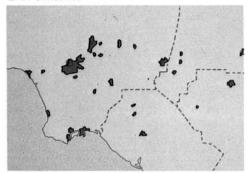

LA 1900

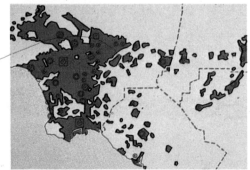

LA 1925

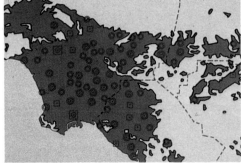

LA 1950

LA 1975

An Anglo-American homage to the Big Orange, a Bicentennial tribute to its excesses and excitements, the following pages hint at the scale, vitality, squalour and style of this unique city. In the

*Is it true what they say about Los Angeles, that
Los Angeles is erratic,
That in the sweet national symphony of common
sense Los Angeles is static?
Yes, it is true. Los Angeles is not only erratic, not
only erotic;
Los Angeles is crotchety, centrifugal, vertiginous,
esoteric and exotic.
Many people blame the movies and the movie-
makers for Los Angeles' emotional rumpus,
But they are mistaken; it is the compass.
Certainly Los Angeles is a cloudburst of non-
sequiturs, and of logic a drouth,
But what can you expect of a city that is laid out
east and west, instead of north and south?
(From 'Don't Shoot Los Angeles' by Ogden Nash)*

Bertrand Russell once told Duncan Aikman that 'Los Angeles represents the ultimate segregation of the unfit!' This collection of observations, vignettes, opinions and reactions set within an intensely visual commentary has purposely been prepared largely by permanent 'unfit' residents of Los Angeles, who get considerable pleasure out of living in this extraordinary city.

We are attempting a thesis which probably, at first sight, is as confusing as the city it endeavours to represent. Los Angeles is a city one defends, not from a traditional standpoint of instant coherence and romantic immediacy like Renaissance Florence or the Bastide towns of France, but as a city of gradual discovery and grandiose excess. If we succeed in peeling a few layers from the popular misconceptions — so much the better.

This vast expanse of urban sprawl, linked by a mesh of asphalt spaghetti with a landtake 70 miles square, has occasioned waspish and hostile comments from the outside. The great American commonplace, Smogsville, a body without a navel, 70 suburbs in search of a city, Tinsel-town, LA the great big freeway — its size and seeming anonymity make every one of these comments legitimate in its own right. What is more fascinating is the power-ful imagery in the city which transcends this abuse, continues to fascinate, break rules, pose problems and solve them, in a constant theatre of hope, retribution, avarice and decay.

The real American knows no problem in-capable of solution and to me Los Angeles is the last frontier town. It still has a powerful will to succeed with its own resources. What lends a unique quality to life in the city is the ethic of conspicuous consumption and the range of options

available to most of the residents with this outlook. But not all Los Angelenos have the kind of personal mobility and resources necessary for such choice. Fifteen per cent of households in LA don't own cars, and this figure is higher in the ghettos of east LA and Watts. To many people, particularly the poor and the elderly, the 'earthly paradise' recedes constantly beyond their grasp. Minority groups continue to suffer — poverty and decades of dis-crimination have contained the blacks and Chicanos to inner-city enclaves. The hard core ghetto remains unchanged, despite massive anti-poverty programmes. Thus, 15 years after the Watts riots of 1965, poverty, crime and despair are still rampant. The barrios of East Los Angeles remain, and the frustration and anger are still expressed in the graffiti and murals that abound in these communities.

It is a minefield for a planning strategy that has to succeed. It is already a multi-centred city, and this should be sustained and reinforced. The public transport system must start to make more sense. Travelling times have to be minimised. Its bright lining consists of its low density -- 6 200 people per square mile compared with Chicago's 15 000 - and its Mediterranean climate, with sunshine gen-erated 250 days of the year, miles of beaches and the San Bernadino and San Gabriel mountain ranges insulating the region climatically.

My own hypnotic love for LA was conditioned early in life by the unlikely combination of Charles and Ray Eames, the movie business and the Brooklyn Dodgers. The first cause is easy to explain -- Charles and Ray Eames personify design as it should be practised. Timelessness, style, wit, rigour and quality. The movies signify a chronic case of never outgrowing Flash Gordon and the Saturday morning flea-pit. The Dodgers' attraction is altogether a product of Sandy Koufax and the great Series of 1965. When they took the trip from New York to Los Angeles in 1958, so did I. Surely Koufax, Charles and Ray Eames and Billy Wilder couldn't all be wrong . . . and now after many years digging for gold, I am sure they were right.

I am also sure that there is something in Jack Smith's view that the English have a curious affi-nity with the city. He reckons the New Yorker is the most bilious critic, because he is obsessed with envy. The French are the most supercilious because they suffer from a national sense of divine super-iority. The English are the most amusing, because they are the only ones who can survive the cultural shock of LA without losing their sense of humour.

LOS ANGELES

LA 1857

continuous repetition of the multiple image, the camera's eye offers a captivating recreation of that laboratory of the senses – the Los Angeles experience.

More recently I have felt the need to check more carefully two assumptions that were being pushed fairly regularly down my throat, that LA as a prototype for future cities leaves one pessimistic and disheartened about the future, and that secondly, my own personal trauma of the times, Milton Keynes (a minnow of 49 square miles compared to LA's 490), because of its grid mesh and mobility patterns, had been flatteringly or unflatteringly and very inconclusively likened to the Big Orange. If one could throw in the sea, the sun, the strip and the service industry of LA, I would be more convinced.

This personal pilgrimage, USC's 100th Year Anniversary, John Nicolais' slide collection and a rush of blood to the head by the Faculty at USC Department of Architecture, conspired to produce a loosefit meander through aspects of the city that fascinated us all. The word that cropped up in early discussions of the project was continually 'excess'. It seemed impossible to portray successfully the size of the fragments. How can you illustrate the building boom that produces 300 000 bungalows in 20 years, show 20 000 Gingerbreads or 1 000 Hansel and Gretels? Whether it is a forest fire or earthquakes, floods or the length of beaches, kitsch entrances or street singing, endless strip or 'wonder wheels', barbecues or bums, LA provides an indigestible excess.

My first view of an LAPD Administrative Report seemed modest by American crime standards, until I suddenly realised it was a weekly sheet and not an annual total. Homicides from January to October 1979 were running at a steady 569, forcible rapes 2 032, robbery 14 841, aggravated assault 14 985, burglary 50 227 — which gives a rather positive indication that the LAPD doesn't just hand out speeding tickets.

The bizarre and the banal meet shoulder to shoulder on every trip with the exquisite and the unique. The multiple faces of the city have led to many pages devoted to a visual itinerary. The sections endeavour to summarise three facets. *LA Morphology* seeks to establish scale, size, the patterns of movement and servicing, the predominant pattern of development, the political framework of the city, its growth and physical characteristics. *LA Architecture* establishes the pattern of an imported civilisation, its eclectic tradition from the Puebelo origins, the European invasion, the great Source architects, the romantic mission style, the neglected rational tradition, the unique contribution in domestic housing, the courtyards, the case

Contemporary LA

studies, the experimental tracts, the imprint of the corporate offices and the multi-directional aspects of the present generation.

Finally, *LA Culture* embraces the excesses and the excitement in the 'Iconology of the Mundane', be it popular architecture or popular art. Entertainment and tourism or the living and the dead. The Southern Californian cult of the physical is emphasised by our visual images. 'The Southern Californian cult of the body' writes Farnsworth Crowder, 'snubs tradition, formality and dignity. Sunbathing, nudity, bare heads, open neck shirts are not imposed by cranks, they are dictated by the sun.' Health consciousness is extreme, reflected in the medical profession and in the prevalence of quackery, pseudo-science and cultism. The climate is so entirely congenial to the American athletics mania that sports flourish and champions are a major product.

Body awareness is of course heightened for many women by the presence of the movies and one sees glamour attempted in the most unexpected corners and on the most improbable faces and figures, until as one draws closer and closer to Hollywood and Vine the effect becomes positively bizarre. All of which might be crudely summed up by saying that there is an inevitable, intrinsic, subtropical drive backed by the authority of the land itself to 'go native' physiologically. This drive, however, is just sufficiently qualified that it doesn't push people into complete intellectual and moral laxity.

Herein lies California's singularity, her magic, her enormous appeal to outsiders and her hold upon her residents!

That final definition may satisfy some, but to me the conclusive quotation is from another Englishman, D H Lawrence, whose words on LA, which he wrote on a card to a friend, still ring true today: 'LA is silly — much motoring, me rather tired and vague about it. California is a queer place in a way, it has turned its back on the world and looks into the void Pacific. It is absolutely selfish, very empty but not false, and at least not full of false effort. I don't want to live here, but a stay here rather amuses me. It is a sort of "crazy sensible." ' The 'crazy' of Lawrence's notes consists of the old traditions incongruously retained; the 'sensible' consists of the new fresh growth. Perhaps it will always retain something — its sort of 'crazy sensible'. I hope so!!!

Derek Walker

LA 1850 (p: LA Department of Water and Power)

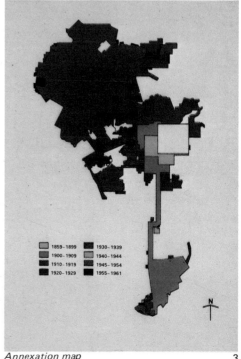

1859–1899	1930–1939
1900–1909	1940–1944
1910–1919	1945–1954
1920–1929	1955–1961

Annexation map

3

1. THE MORPHOLOGY OF LOS ANGELES

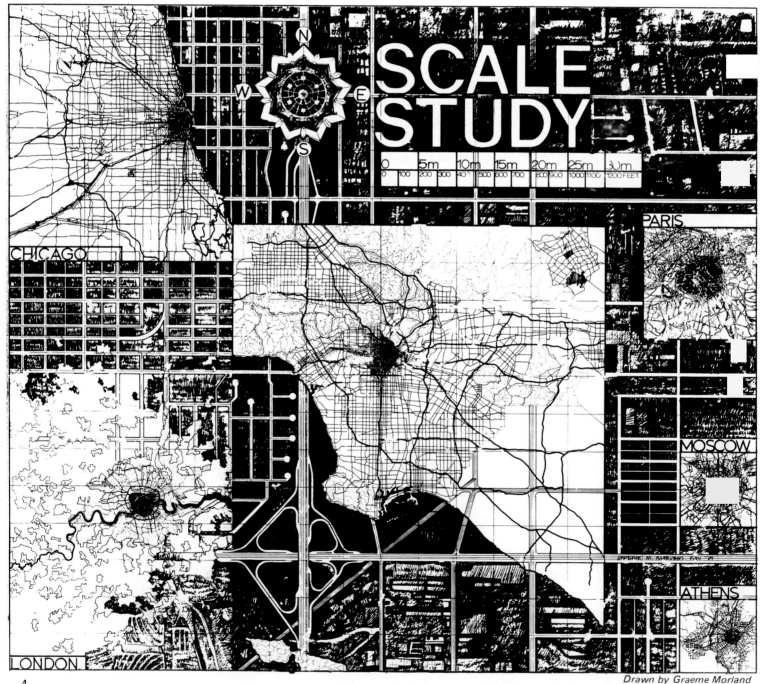

SCALE STUDY

| 0 | 5m | 10m | 15m | 20m | 25m | 30m |
| 0 | 100 200 300 | 400 500 600 700 | 800 900 1000 1100 | 1200 FEET |

CHICAGO

PARIS

MOSCOW

ATHENS

LONDON

Drawn by Graeme Morland

Sam Hurst

CONTRADICTIONS: LA 1930–1980

A DIALECTICAL ANALYSIS

When it is impossible for the productive forces to develop without a change in the relations of production, then the change in the relations of production plays the principal and decisive role.   Mao

... one is led almost automatically to the discovery of what may well be the 'drama' of architecture today: that is, to see architecture obliged to return to **pure architecture***, to form without utopia; in the best cases, to sublime uselessness.*   Tafuri

As the final quarter of this 20th-century ballgame begins the score might well be reported, Exxon 118– the People 2.[1]

The half-century span of this piece can be characterised by its contradictions; essentially they are contradictions between ideals and practice, between public goals widely acknowledged and powerful private interests realised over five decades of depression, war, boom, war and inflation. Pressed by the forces of a demand-driven economy and expanding population, growth has been rapid, upward and outward, exploiting available land, wasting the centre and straining to the breaking point urban systems that were never fully developed in this young city.

For architects, the half-century represents the professional life span of men like Neutra, Ain, Alexander and Able, Eames, Entenza and Ellwood, Jones and Smith. Solid in their work, often inspired and sometimes brilliant, they were unable to alter the shape of the physical environment significantly or to divert the impact of change, because they could not affect the fundamental relations of production which allow architecture to serve the public need. Their notable individual achievements seem lost in the sprawl of unplanned building, save to the dedicated student or visitor who seeks them out. And their considerable social commitments seem dissipated by lack of organised professional effort.

The issues facing this generation of architects are not those of style or technology, although these are neglected. Rather they are issues of control, distribution and conservation. Who controls building? How can architects' services and built resources be better distributed? How can human and material energies be conserved for the common good? Debates about style are diverting and the benefits of our sophisticated high technology lie beyond the reach of most in a construction industry that does not reward inventiveness or pass the savings of mass production on to the consumers of building.

Paradoxically, the new tasks given to architecture are something besides or beyond architecture.   Tafuri

The social message of Baldwin Hills Village, a collaboration of Robert Alexander and Clarence Stein (1942),[2] the simple elegance of Channel Heights Housing by Neutra (1943) and the beautifully reasoned logic of the techno-houses of Eames, Jones, Killingsworth and Koenig are lost in the midst of housing built not for use but for investment.[3] The pristinely luxurious high buildings which now mark the centre of our city are testimony both to the skill of Martin, Periera and Luckman, and to corporate power and ego, but they interface with the blight and vacancy of Broadway and Spring St, and adjoin the barren Bunker Hill Redevelopment, a 20-year hole in the ground.[4] Nowhere is the disparity of development more stridently obvious than in East Los Angeles, a short mile away. There, anger and pride and cultural identity assert themselves as Mexican-Americans struggle for a decent environment.

The social costs of disparity, of blight at the centre and over-extended systems of transportation, schooling, police and fire protection, are now being assessed and the public is fighting back. Learning from the urban upheavals of the 1960s and the anti-war movement of the 1970s, the consumers of building are getting organised. That reality is the dominant force of 1979, often negative, but capable of positive direction. The shape of that force reflects the political response to the contradictions of 50 years of largely unplanned and exploitative development, and its potential for change has to be recognised.

Driven by inflation, a chronic shortage of housing, and a desire to have some participation in the building of their surrounds, the people have learned to use the legal remedies and the political instruments of their democratic system. The following list demonstrates the effects of their initiatives:

—environmental impact studies have drawn attention to the adverse physical and social affects of land use and building decisions, and have stopped airports, nuclear plants and liquid gas terminals;
—the state coastal zoning act has placed control of coastal development in public hands and now mandates coastal housing for those of moderate income;
—freeway building has been slowed, diverted and sometimes stopped where its destructive effects on communities are demonstrated;
—state and local energy audit programmes require accountability by architects for energy consumption in buildings and a State Office of Appropriate Technology leads in reassessment of our habits;
—the Southern California Chapter of AIA is suing the city over the issue of the Central Library, and the Northern

California Chapter is proposing a ballot initiative to limit building height in San Francisco;
—rent control has been imposed by public referendum in El Monte and in Santa Monica and by council action in Los Angeles;
—tenants' rights have been affirmed by local ordinance and are pressed at the state level;
—child tenant rights have been won and open housing mandated in Santa Monica;
—condominium conversion has been frozen or controlled in many areas.

One must ask, 'What is the role of the architect in these events? What will be their impact on his work?' In spite of actions cited above and notable individual contributions of public service, the profession's organised weight remains largely apolitical, if not asocial. Our traditional preoccupation with the form and technology of design leaves little room for the intrusion of social values or political strategies and the architect's aversion to public conflict most often places him on the periphery of activist movements. Many worthy efforts by volunteer architect groups, eg the re-development of Hollywood,[5] represent planning without strategy, power or money. Generally, the architect remains the employed agent in the development process, content to bring narrow professional competence to bear on that process. His essential disengagement from the front-end decisions having wide public environmental consequences is his personal contradiction.

The recent exhibition around the work of *The Los Angeles 12* presumed to show the direction of our most talented designers of the new generation. It squarely places the values of 'Design'/LA/1979.[6] There is little room in such a show for achievements in social and political organisation for a better environment. It challenges the principles of the Modern Movement without offering clear or positive alternatives, as it celebrates style and confusion, which is somehow regarded as more humane than reason. It reflects the confusion of goals in education and in practice.

In this vital, booming city—scarcely a million in 1930 and now second largest metropolitan centre in the nation—blessed with nature's full endowment, how can the public interest be better served by the architect? It can be only by his direct acknowledgement of the forces of the economic and social system within which he lives and works and by his commitment to open that system to the democratic processes idealised in our history. If he has neither the time nor the passion for such a struggle, events will move without significant change in the oppressive quality of the built environment. Waste, pollution, blight and consuming growth may continue to be our lot, or change may come at the hand of others who are less pretentious in their claims.

The Exxon metaphor is useful to illuminate the conflicting nature of present events, to identify the battleground. Fuelled by inflation in the energy field, the national economy is being subjected to federal intervention of all kinds, aimed at slowing the flow of money and credit. The resultant effect is most directly felt in building, especially in home building. With the public taste for fiscal austerity and the near bankruptcy of some city and county governments, one can foresee little building in the public sector. As sheltered investment in the private sector continues and average home costs in the city reach $100000, one can expect increased disparity between the real needs of people and activities in the building market. We cannot play 'racquet ball' 24 hours a day. Children cannot be privately financed or enjoying public tax remission in 'alternative schools', to avoid integration. Young marrieds with children cannot buy condominiums or share the genteel suburban environs of 'new towns' like Valencia and Westlake.[7] And freeways cannot indefinitely support more cars or the air more emissions. People do perceive these realities and want change.

Some change will be mandated by government. It can either perpetuate the bureaucratic modes of problem-solving or respond to creative influences. So stated is the ultimate contradiction: *is government a reliable defender of the public interest?* In times of depression and war it has often performed that way. Vietnam, Watergate and the fuel crisis with its windfall profits have shaken public confidence, and many do not go to the polls.

What a time for architects to enter the public debate! When has the substance of public need been better suited to their interest and training? *Where is the architect in the community?* He will find 'the community' when he can identify himself with its collective interests, when he can find a way of working in the activity of community building, a people's enterprise. What would come if young architects really organised a public interest practice? What would we change if we could alter the relations of production?

In simple terms the elements of production are *land*, *labour*, *material* and *capital*. The forces of production may be seen as *need*, *power* and *profit*. Too long we have suffered these forces operating in the free climate of Southern California in service of the dictum of 'speed, greed and exploitation', extravagantly wasteful of resources which are now seen as limited. Social and environmental conditions call upon us to practise an architecture of conservation, conserving both human and natural resources in the interest of a better future. People want it. Acting in their interest, the government will mandate it. Our challenge is to earn a place in the process, acquiring power by working to identify real need, communicating with the architect's skills of analysis and conception to show a better way, challenging destructive forces and actors, generating a positive collective will.

Is the battle worth joining? The early struggle for modern architecture in California provides some models. Pioneer modernists fought and seemed to enjoy the battle. Some died poor. We honour the Greene brothers for the complete integrity of their work, Gill for his structural inventiveness and the 'bare honesty' of his expression. Schindler's manipulations of space and Neutra's mastery of land and site inspired many who followed. It is not disparaging to say that their work was usually unconnected, consisting of solo performances whose lessons were lost on the public mind. Neutra's Bell Avenue Experimental School (1935) would be unknown to the current LA School Board and probably disallowed.[8]

Our opportunities do lie 'beyond architecture', certainly beyond style and technology. The architect may soil himself in social and political struggle. That risk is worth taking for the beauty and power and life-potential of this place we call Los Angeles. This 'island' in the California sun is yet to be known.

Santa Monica Beach

Eames House

Case Study – Koenig

X100 1956 – Jones

Schindler House

Skyline LA

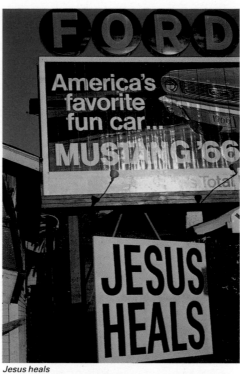

Jesus heals

Street art East LA

Downtown LA

Union Bank LA

United California Bank

Notes

1 Currently reported third quarter earnings, Exxon up 118%

2 See an analysis of Baldwin Hills Village by Richard Berry, *Arts and Architecture.*

3 See Charles Eames House, Los Angeles, and series of Case Study Houses, *Arts and Architecture,* John Entenza, Editor, 1940s.

4 See published reports and plans of Los Angeles Community Redevelopment Agency, Bunker Hill.

5 See report of the SCCAIA Urban Design Committee, Chapter Newsletter, 1979.

6 See exhibition announcement, *The Los Angeles 12* 1979.

7 See regional maps of metropolitan Los Angeles.

8 See *Five California Architects*, Esther McCoy, Reinhold, 1960; and *Architects on Architecture*, New Directions in America, Paul Heyer, Walker and Co, 1966.

LA AERIALS

Wilshire / Santa Monica 1924

Wilshire / Santa Monica 1968

Westwood Village 1930

Westwood Village 1964

Forest Lawn 1926

Colorado 8.30 am January 1 1938

Long Beach outer harbour

Long Beach drilling island

Doheny Ranch Beverly Hills 1960

San Diego Freeway from PICO

Santa Monica Pier

Olympic Opening 1932

9

We are indebted to the Department of Geography at UCLA who have enabled us to use photographs from the Spence Collection, which they hold within the Department, and to the Environmental Systems Research Institute for the satellite photographs of LA.

LA Harbours

Wilshire Centre from Griffith Park

Harbour Freeway corridor looking West

Santa Monica harbour interchange

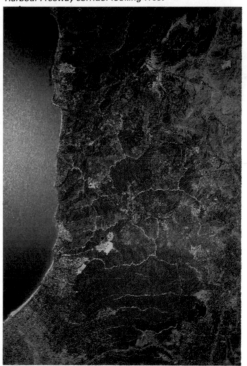

Palos Verdes Hills

LA view from Griffith Park

Graeme Morland
MOVEMENT SYSTEMS

TRANSPORTATION AND CIRCULATION WITHIN THE LOS ANGELES AREA

The socio-economic and environmental prosperity of Los Angeles and its supporting activity centres depends heavily on the capability and adequacy of the transportation services available. Improvements in the existing transit systems must be implemented if the objectives of the community goals programmes are to thrive.

The focus of transportation planning over the past 20 years has been the development of the freeways and their potential for achieving continuous flow circulation. However, despite the sophistication of the LA freeway network with all its complex of valves and interchanges, the problems arising from the proliferation of private vehicles have established the ironic paradox between support system capability and environmental by-product. In recognition of this dichotomy, it is now acknowledged that freeways and autos in their present form are only a partial answer to the solution of mass urban transportation.

It is now clearly evident that a system of diverse capability is essential to cope with the varied needs of individual and mass commuter pattern and intensity, rather than a 'gross' system attempting to sustain all to the majority peak demand. To this end Los Angeles is now committed to the development of a balanced (multiple service) public transit system responsive to local and metropolitan needs.

Historical Setting

The first major land boom in Los Angeles occurred in 1868 with the opening of a railroad line from Los Angeles to the Port of San Pedro. The first transit line in Los Angeles was the Spring and West Sixth St Railroad, opened in 1874, and extending two and a half miles. Other horsedrawn car lines were soon installed with a line along Main Street to the present Exposition Park opened in 1877.

By 1885 some of the lines were being replaced by cable cars and Angel's Flight, a funicular cable system, was opened in 1901 and remained in operation until the 1860s. In 1888 the Pico Street electric line was opened to serve new housing development on Pico. This was followed by the opening of several other electric lines, most of which were installed by private developers to promote the sale of land and property. The ensuing land marketing techniques connected with early public rail transit led primarily to what is provocatively termed suburban sprawl. The sub-division of Santa Monica occurred within six months of the opening of the Santa Monica line from Downtown Los Angeles.

In 1890 the predecessor of the Los Angeles Railway was incorporated to purchase all of the cable car lines for conversion to electric. In 1898 the Southern Pacific Railroad (Huntington) purchased the Los Angeles Railway and all other remaining competitive streetcar lines. By 1910, Huntington had expanded his monopoly to some 377 miles of service and within five years to 650 miles. At the same time the Pacific Electric Interurban railroad was expanding throughout Southern California, linking downtown LA with San Bernardino and Riverside in the east, and the coastline on the west.

Streetcar and Pacific Electric Cars ran side by side through most downtown streets with heavy service on Broadway, Spring, Hill and Main. As the communities along Pacific Electric Lines developed, the number of grade crossings increased; this, coupled with the increasing popularity of private automobiles, brought about congestion, more accidents and eventually a general deterioration in rail services.

A severe drop in patronage was further experienced in 1915 with the proliferation of Jitney service in the Los Angeles area. Although the railroads were able to get severe restrictive laws passed to eliminate Jitney competition, the ensuing period saw the initiation of the first bus line operations, which in conjunction with speed restrictions imposed on rail service due to congestion and traffic conflicts, hastened the collapse of the streetcar system. As bus service increased, there were several competing bus companies in Los Angeles. Most of these merged and were included in the Southern California Rapid Transit District, the principal bus operator in the Los Angeles region at present. Many of the bus lines inherited the same routes as the old streetcar system and the service patterns remained very similar.

Although the buses that replaced the street cars were modern and comfortable they could not compete with the speed or convenience afforded by the private automobile, and before long the public transport system was demoted to a primarily back-up system. As ridership dropped, routes were abandoned, and earlier provisions for bus turn-offs or lay-by platforms on a non-flourishing freeway network have since been predominantly dropped in favour of increased driving lanes.

Since World War II the expansion of the freeway system and the growth and development of Los Angeles and other regional centres in accordance with the adopted city centres plan, have focused attention on the ever-increasing volume of private automobiles as the predominant mode of travel in Los Angeles. Although the total number of persons entering and leaving the central city has not increased dramatically over the past ten years, decreases in vehicle occupancy have resulted in a net increase in the number of vehicles using the freeways.

Numerous studies have been undertaken calling for a comprehensive public transportation network, and investigation of alternative transit modes. Some of these proposals have addressed the employment of exclusive bus lanes on freeways, use of private railway corridors and flood control channels, monorails or other guide-rail systems, and subways. Until 1974 public endorsement to generate tax revenues to support alternative public transit modes could not be mustered, but the last five years have seen an increasing attitudinal shift, which recognises the vulnerability of the prevailing system in its dependence on gasolene.

The romance between Los Angeles and the automobile is not only being questioned but is now facing its severest test.

Existing Transportation and Circulation

Contrary to popular opinion, the evidence of a viable public transport system in Los Angeles is becoming clear. The reality of public dependence on the existing system was underlined when recent transit strikes were coupled with a prevailing gasolene shortage.

The Southern California Rapid Transport District (SCRTD) operates approximately 12,000 one-way bus trips daily, into, out of, or through downtown Los Angeles. In the afternoon peak hour the highest volume is on Hill Street, between Eighth Street and Fifth Street with 147 buses per hour, 84 local and 63 freeway travelling north; southbound lanes in the same location carry 51 buses in the same peak hour.

In addition to the regular bus route service, SCRTD initiated a Park and Ride service in 1974 which consists of 12 routes comprising over 40 bus trips serving 1,500 persons daily. Characteristic of this service is the one stop at point of origin and many stops at points of destination within downtown. Taxis provide destination oriented service to and from the downtown area in addition to bus and mini-bus operations. However, this service has diminished in recent years due to the increasing success of mini-bus operations.

Greyhound and Continental Trailways offer inter-city bus service to downtown Los Angeles. Patronage is at a maximum during weekend periods, in contrast to SCRTD use; approximately 7,000 arrivals and departures are handled per weekend day from the downtown terminals.

Other transit systems in Los Angeles include a shuttle service operating to and from Los Angeles International Airport (LAX) and principal downtown locations, hotels, bus depots, convention centre etc. Approximately 31,000–35,000 persons per month use this service. Intercity rail service is operated by Amtrak, between San Diego and Los Angeles, Union Station. This serves as a commuter rail service for residents of south east Los Angeles, Orange and San Diego counties.

Another successful form of many-to-one transit service is the van pool, where the passenger is delivered directly to his destination. Gasolene shortage and increased costs have made this programme very attractive. Car pool programmes are also in operation with efforts to solicit private sector participation and encourage high occupancy of vehicles. To this end efforts have been made to develop exclusive bus, van and car pool lanes on the freeways. There is enough evidence to demonstrate that Los Angeles is now prepared to face the challenge of developing a responsive, multiple-service transit system.

To underline this commitment, the regional transit development programme has been inaugurated to orchestrate all local agencies to work in concert towards the development of an integrated, co-ordinated, public transit programme. The major components of the programme to be interfaced are the following:

1 *Transportation System Management.* An on-going programme to upgrade the existing fleet of buses and to modernise or construct fleet operating services and public transit facilities.

2 *Bus on Freeway Programme.* This programme calls for the extension of the San Bernardino busway to Union Station in downtown Los Angeles and the development of an additional 36 miles of exclusive public transit lanes on the Santa Ana, Harbour and proposed Century freeways. In addition, 21 new stations will be constructed with ancillary parking facilities.

3 *Downtown People Mover.* The guideway shuttle system will function as a key element of the regional transit system by providing ease of connection between activity centres in Los Angeles and rail and bus terminals. The people mover will not only facilitate connections between centres, ie Convention Center and major Hotels, but will serve as a glue acting on present disparate elements of the city.

4 *Regional Core, Rapid Transit Starter Line.* The starter line will begin at Union Station, the nucleus of the regional transit system, where connections with the people mover, Amtrak, freeway bus transit and local bus service and taxi operations are made. The proposed machine-bored subway system will extend 18 miles, from Union Station, through the central business district, along Wilshire Boulevard, through Hollywood to North Hollywood. It is expected to carry some 15,000 passengers per hour in both directions, with 16 new stations along the route, and the potential for stimulating economic growth and development at each connection.

Bibliography

1 Arthur B Gallion, *The Urban Pattern. City Planning and Design*

2 CRA, *Moving People in Los Angeles: Summary Report of the Los Angeles Circulation/Distribution Programme*

3 ARCO, *Ideas on Public Transportation*

4 *LA Architect* (October 1979)

Long Beach harbour

Air pollution averages 1973–75

Noise contours 1970

LAX airport

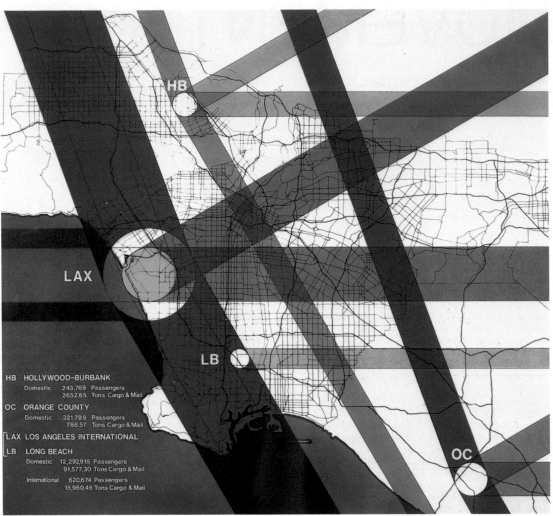

HB **HOLLYWOOD–BURBANK**
   Domestic   243,769 Passengers
              2652,65 Tons Cargo & Mail

OC **ORANGE COUNTY**
   Domestic   321,789 Passengers
              788,57 Tons Cargo & Mail

LAX **LOS ANGELES INTERNATIONAL**

LB **LONG BEACH**
   Domestic   12,292,915 Passengers
              91,577,30 Tons Cargo & Mail

   International   620,674 Passengers
                  15,960,45 Tons Cargo & Mail

Air traffic diagram

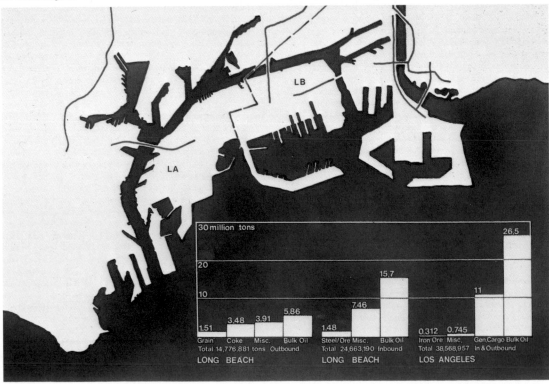

Ocean bound commerce

30 million tons									
						15,7			26.5
20									
10					7.46			11	
	3.48	3.91	5,86						
1.51				1.48			0.312	0.745	
Grain	Coke	Misc.	Bulk Oil	Steel/Ore	Misc.	Bulk Oil	Iron Ore	Misc.	Gen.Cargo Bulk Oil
Total 14,776,881 tons Outbound				Total 24,663,190 Inbound			Total 38,568,957 In & Outbound		
LONG BEACH				LONG BEACH			LOS ANGELES		

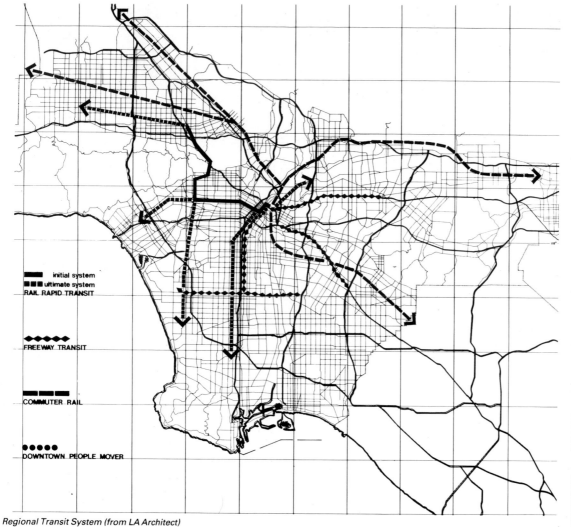

initial system
RAIL RAPID TRANSIT ■■■ ultimate system

◆◆◆ FREEWAY TRANSIT

▬ ▬ ▬ COMMUTER RAIL

●●●● DOWNTOWN PEOPLE MOVER

Regional Transit System (from LA Architect)

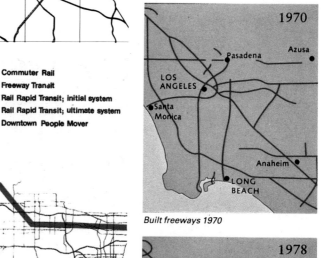

━━━ Commuter Rail
━━━ Freeway Transit
━━━ Rail Rapid Transit; initial system
━━━ Rail Rapid Transit; ultimate system
━━━ Downtown People Mover

Traffic flow LA

1951

Azusa
Pasadena
LOS ANGELES
Santa Monica
Anaheim
LONG BEACH

Source:
Southern California AAA

Built freeways 1950

1960

Azusa
Pasadena
LOS ANGELES
Santa Monica
Anaheim
LONG BEACH

Built freeways 1960

1970

Pasadena   Azusa
LOS ANGELES
Santa Monica
Anaheim
LONG BEACH

Built freeways 1970

1978

Azusa
Pasadena
LOS ANGELES
Santa Monica
Anaheim
LONG BEACH

Built freeways 1978

Long Beach Freeway (7) (N–S), Pamona Freeway (60) (E–W), at Monterey Park

Harbour Freeway (11) (N–S), Santa Monica Freeway (10) (E–W), at LA

Santa Monica Freeway (5) (N–S), San Bernardino Freeway (10) (E–W), at LA

Harbour Freeway (11) (N–S), Hollywood Freeway (101) (E–W), at LA

Helicopter patrol LAPD

Cal Tran operations room

University bus station

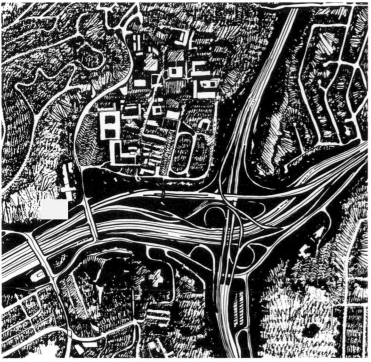

Long Beach Freeway Interchange (7) (N–S), San Bernardino Freeway (10) (E–W), East LA

Golden State Freeway (5) N–S), Foothill Freeway (210) (E–W), San Fernando

Golden State Freeway (5) (N–S), Route 11b Pacoima

San Diego Freeway (405) (N–S), Santa Monica Freeway (10) (E–W), Santa Monica

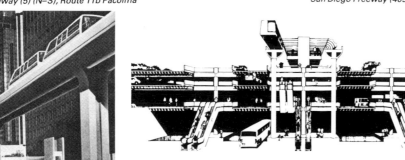

LA Downtown people mover

Union Station Bus and Carpool Auto Intercept

People mover route

17

Derek Walker
INDUSTRY AND EMPLOYMENT

Aerospace industry

LA River

Industrial relaxation!

View down to Long Beach

Western truck exchange

The most powerful visual account of Los Angeles' employment options is carried in the superb *Atlas of California* published in 1979 by The Pacific Book Center in Culver City, on which the following figures and facts are based.

Though historically Los Angeles has been dominated by oil, aircraft and space programmes, the movie industry and agriculture, it is second only to New York in apparel manufacture, and has a construction industry of sufficient scale to cope with the most dynamic growth point in American settlement history, employing, as it does, 5% of the whole private sector work force. Its port facilities handle 60,000,000 tons per year. Private and Government services together constitute close to a third of the employment. One fifth of the workforce in the private sector is engaged in performing services and half the Governmental workers are similarly employed, mostly in Education and Health.

Over eighty radio stations operate in the Los Angeles area, ranging in content from Beautiful Music via Progressive Jazz to the Spanish language and news and talk shows. There are also 13 television stations, the most profitable being owned by CBS, NBC and ABC respectively. Both CBS and ABC have moved their entertainment division to Los Angeles, where nearly half of the 32,000 people working in movie production were making pictures for television.

Wholesale trade ranks second to New York, and in 1972 sales values were in the region of 32,500 million dollars. Retail centres abound and 40 in the Los Angeles area have turnovers in excess of 100 million dollars in retail sales per annum. Over ten of these are in excess of 2,000 million dollars. An interesting exercise is charting the million dollar corporations; 21 industrials had sales or revenue in excess of one billion dollars in 1977.

A collection of lists is probably more revealing than a written commentary; it provides both volume and scale. What it doesn't do is underline Los Angeles' popular boast that if you want anything, but *anything*, from a high quality fine finish paint job to a hand crafted low rider, a Paris original or a dust free plastic tent, 'fetish finish' is available ... at a price.

Million Dollar Corporations

There are 582 million dollar Corporations in Los Angeles. Sixty-three headquartered in Los Angeles and Orange Counties, have revenues ranging from $145 million to $20.18 billion. 21 industrials had sales or revenues of more than a billion dollars in 1977. Seven were oil companies (Standard, Atlantic Richfield, Union, Occidental, Getty, Signal and Reserve): five were defence-related industries (Litton, Lockheed, Teledyne, Northrop and Hewlett Packard): three were food and drug companies (Foremost-McKesson, Carnation and Del Monte).

Employment in Leading Manufacturing Industries, 1975

Transportation Equipment. 193,000 people employed in: Aircraft, Missiles and Space Vehicles, Motor Vehicles.

Electric and Electronic Equipment. 123,000 people employed in: Communications Equipment, Electronic Components, Lighting and Wiring.

Machinery other than Electrical. 103,000 people employed in: Office Machines and Computers, General Industrial Machinery, Construction and Oil Field Machinery.

Food and Kindred Products. In excess of 56,000 people employed in: Preserved Fruits and Vegetables, Bakery Products, Beverages.

Fabricated Metal Products. 85,000 people employed in: Structural Metal Products, Cutlery, Hand Tools and Hardware, Screw Machine Products.

Printing and Publishing. 53,000 people employed in: Newspapers, Commercial Printing, Periodicals.

Apparel and Textile Products. 69,000 people employed in: Women's Apparel, Men's Apparel, Miscellaneous Textile Products.

Instruments and Related Products. 32,000 people employed in: Measuring and Control Devices, Medical Instruments and Supplies, Engineering and Scientific Instruments.

General Aviation

26,000 private aircraft were licensed in California in 1976, with 16 million take-offs and landings at the 314 airfields. Heaviest volume of traffic – Orange County with 1,700 operations a day.

Los Angeles Airports: daily flight operations

Santa Susana	274	Hawthorne	515
Whiteman	274	Orange County	1699
El Monte	573	Torrance	1205
Brackett	597	Santa Monica	701
Ontario	499	LA International	1244
Chino	567	Ventura County	507
Fullerton	658	Van Nuys	1610
Meadowlark	247	Hollywood-Burbank	628
Long Beach	1534	Riverside	349
Compton	438	Skylark	548

Employment diagram (from the Atlas of California)

- Agriculture, forestry, fisheries
- Finance, insurance, real estate
- Transport, utilities, communication
- Government
- Services
- Retail trade
- Wholesale trade
- Manufacturing
- Construction

100%

OIL

Set construction

Oil in your garden

Long Beach harbour

Industrial blight

Long Beach oil rigs

AEROSPACE

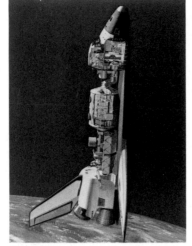

Space shuttle

Space shuttle

Space shuttle Rockwell

Space shuttle Rockwell

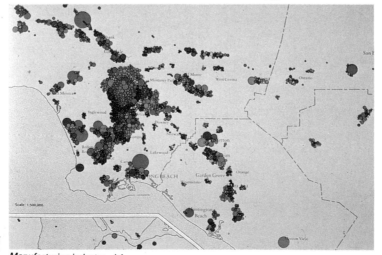

Manufacturing industry – LA

MOVIES

Disneyland

Film studios

Film set

Million Dollar Movie

AGRICULTURE

Orange grove

Flower field

Tuna fleet

Irrigation

Fashion island

19

Dimitry Vergun and Derek Walker
CATASTROPHE LA

Expansive soils, landslides and flooding, tectonic and volcanic hazards, surface erosion, and fire provide five potential natural hazards whose severity ranges from mild to catastrophic – they are physical spectres which have to be negotiated annually in the Los Angeles basin.

Expansive soils contain swelling clays of the illite and montmorillonite groups, which can absorb water. When they do, they expand and often damage human structures. They also lose their internal strength on absorbing water and are likely to deform or slide.

Landslides and floods usually occur from the kind of heavy precipitation which reduces soil strength and produces mass movement. Winter torrents in particular erode adjacent slopes severely, and often trigger slides on built-up residential slopes. In addition, wild fires or construction of buildings and roads alter surface form and promote landsliding, surface run-off and flooding.

Earthquakes are clearly perceived as a hazard by Californians, but two other tectonic dangers – volcanic eruptions and *tsunamis* – are less recognised. *Tsunamis* or tidal waves pose a threat to populated coastal zones and are caused by earthquakes in the Pacific basin. They usually do little damage.

Surface erosion often causes major damage by decreasing the productivity of the soil and its water retention capacity. The transport of eroded materials does further damage – silt in streams damages the habitat for fish and increases the flood potential by clogging drains and canals.

The final scourge of the Los Angeles basin is fire. In 1978 over 10 000 fires were controlled by the California forest fire agencies.

Perhaps to underline the magnitude of these physical hazards it would be appropriate to dwell on two of the most potentially destructive: earthquake and fire.

The seriousness of the fire-problem in Los Angeles County has been well documented. There have been four major fires since 1956, including the most recent which occurred on 23 October, 1978. Each of these incidents has involved large acreage loss in a short period of time (20 000 to 27 000 acres within six to 24 hours). A report is on file which indicates that the entire Santa Monica Mountain area has burned over at least once since 1925. The causes are many but evidence shows that most fires are man-related. Along with the dramatic density-increase in fire-prone areas, use of flammable building materials and poor brush clearance have resulted in tremendous property losses. In the 1961 Bel Air Fire in the Santa Monica Mountains, most of the homes destroyed had either poor brush clearance, flammable wood roofs, or both. Four-hundred eighty-four houses were destroyed of the 2 204 which are threatened.

The implications for the building industry – in particular, the housing construction industry – in Los Angeles County are enormous. Following the October 1978 series of fires, new legislation was introduced which would severely limit the use of certain flammable materials including wood roof shingles and shakes, and certain types of exterior siding, in Fire Zone 4 areas. This legisalation would also limit certain types of vegetation within 1 000 feet of houses.

But even the best preventive measures will not eliminate the threat of major fires. Unique climatic and topographic conditions make the mountainous and adjacent areas natural targets for conflagration. During the period from early spring to late fall, eastern winds occasionally sweep over the outlying desert. When these winds, known as Santa Ana Winds, hit the mountainous areas, conditions become potentially explosive. Coupled with the large amount of available fuel, portions of Los Angeles County present a fire control problem which may be without equal elsewhere in the world.

During Santa Ana conditions, it is not unusual for fires to 'spot' ahead more than 2 miles at a time. For example, a spot fire during the 1961 Bel Air Fire was measured at 1.6 miles ahead of the main fire. All of this leads to a treacherous fire control and suppression problem. Partially due to the high density-increase in the past decade, fire-protection water systems in much of the mountainous areas are generally substandard and in some areas totally inadequate.

October 23, 1978. Several wildland fires of significance occurred in Los Angeles County on this day. A survey of them gives a good indication of the explosive nature of the Los Angeles mountain areas.

At 4:00 am on the morning of the 23rd, a rapid change in the weather occurred. Relative humidity, which had been 65 per cent at 3:00 am, plummeted to 17 per cent and for the next 16 hours remained at or below this level. The high temperature of the day was 80 degrees F at 2:00 pm, while relative humidity at this time was 13 per cent. Northeast winds which had begun to develop at 11:00 pm on the previous night, were by 8:00 am gusting up to 35 MPH and were extremely unstable, varying from northest to southeast by the minute.

The Kanan Fire, the largest of the 14 separate fires occurring on this one day, was first reported at 12:11 pm. It was reported to have crossed the Pacific Coast Highway at 2:27 pm, a distance of approximately 10 miles. During the Kanan Fire, amongst the 2 058 structures in the fire area, 224 houses were damaged or destroyed. In a preliminary survey of those houses damaged or destroyed in the Kanan Fire, information regarding the roofing material is available for 91 per cent. Of those with known roofing material, 38 per cent had wood shingle roofs. Many of the structures in the area were constructed with wood siding or had other negative feature such as exposed eaves or large expanses of glass.

Since 1769 the state has experienced approximately 5 000 earthquakes each year. Most were not destructive but predictions of large earthquakes occur which will centre in California. The Richter scale, commonly used to measure earthquake magnitude, was developed by Charles Richter of the California Institute of Technology. On this scale an earthquake which measures six or more is potentially destructive, and one of seven is considered a major quake.

The shock that rocked the San Fernando Valley in February of 1971 is one of the recent major seismic events. The earthquake had a Richter magnitude of 6.5, resulted in 64 deaths and caused an estimated $511 000 000 in damage. But it could have been worse – the early hour of the shock at 6 am prevented greater loss of life and the dam on Lower Van Norman Lake did not completely fail. Secondary ramifications of the quake included the near dam failure which resulted in the evacuation of a large section of the Valley and more than a thousand landslides triggered by the ground motion.

The problem of designing buildings in an area prone to seismic shocks has, strangely enough, not resulted in an architecture expressive of the problem. Buildings in Los Angeles look to the layman just like buildings anywhere else. To an architect or an engineer, however, there are subtle signs of special problems, particularly if one looks closely at buildings, during construction. For example, today one would not see any unreinforced masonry buildings being built, such as were common prior to 1933 Long Beach earthquake. They have been found extremely susceptible to total or partial collapse.

As a result of the 1933 earthquake, a ban on buildings over 160 feet in height was imposed in Los Angeles, until research in the dynamic response of multistorey structures in the 1950s showed that height in itself was not a danger and the ban was lifted. Of course much research has been carried out at Stanford and Berkeley on the seismic response of buildings in the last 40 years. As a result, California Building Codes, including that of Los Angeles, were the first major codes to put seismic design on a dynamic· rather than static basis. With the advent of computer technology, modelling of the dynamic response of buildings became a design tool for the engineer. Today, any major building that is not uniform in mass distribution, and is irregular in plan is subject to a dynamic analysis before a building permit is issued.

Architectural systems, such as curtain walls, pre-cut walls, elevators, essential piping, etc, are required to be designed to accommodate the movement associated with earthquakes. Such movements may exceed an inch per floor, and result in substantial detailing problems. Buildings must also allow for seismic separation at the property lines so as to preclude the hammering of adjacent buildings. A limitation has been placed on rigid shearwall or x-brand structures; they can only be used for buildings under 160-feet high. Buildings over that height must consist of a complete three-dimensional rigid frame designed to remain ductile in the plastic range. Such frames traditionally have been built of steel, but in recent years techniques have been developed that allow ductile frames to be built of concrete.

Present codes, however, should not be considered definitive. After the failure of several modern structures in the 1971 earthquake, significant code changes have been implemented, with some types of buildings having the design lateral forces increased by 50 per cent in the latest code editions, which are normally revised every three years.

Another interesting aspect of the problem is what to do with the many thousands of unreinforced masonary buildings, considered hazardous to life and limb, that are still used. The Los Angeles City council is presently studying the problem and it is considered likely that such building will be required either to be strengthened for increased earthquake resistance or demolished. The exact course of action to be taken is at present unknown, but will almost certainly involve a major workload on the part of design professionals in the area of Los Angeles in years to come.

Dimitry Vergun, Derek Walker

Bibliography:
Robert Iacopi *Earthquake Country*
Report of the Los Angeles Earthquake Commission: San Fernando Earthquake, February 9, 1971
California Geology, April-May, 1971
Atlas of California. Pacific Book Center, Culver City, California.

Location of major fires, October 23 1978

Forest fire

Flood area, Anaheim

Long Beach earthquake 1933

Long Beach earthquake 1933

Earthquake damage on Freeway

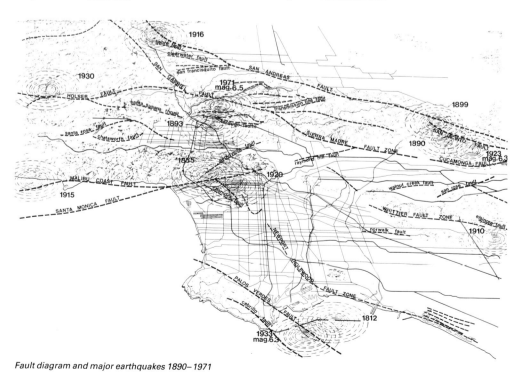

Fault diagram and major earthquakes 1890–1971

Mud slide

Mount Washington slide 69

DEMOGRAPHIC MAPS

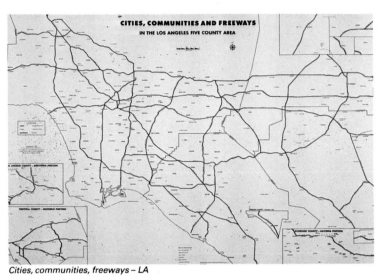

Cities, communities, freeways – LA

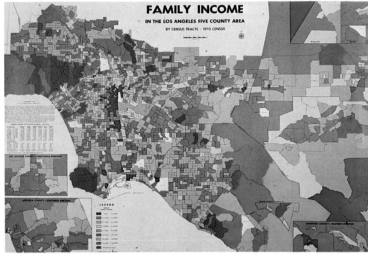

Family income 1970 census

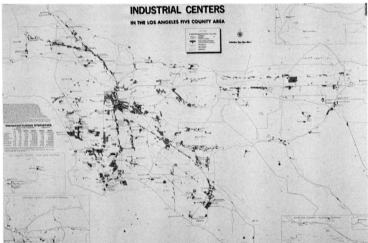

Industrial centres

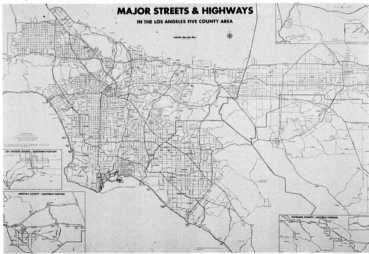

Major streets and highways

Shopping centres

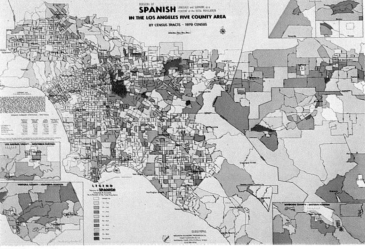

1970 Census Spanish speaking areas

We wish to thank the US Department of Labour and Employment for diagrams from the Urban Atlas, and the Western Economic Research Co, 13037 Ventura Boulevard LA for use of their census.

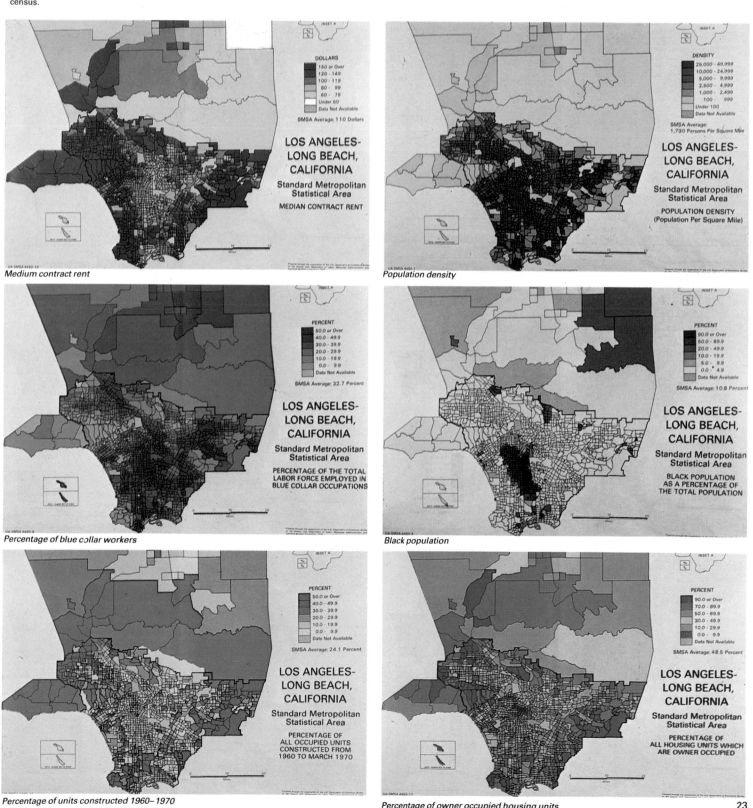

Medium contract rent

Population density

Percentage of blue collar workers

Black population

Percentage of units constructed 1960–1970

Percentage of owner occupied housing units

Eugene Tatum Brookes
VIGNETTE OF THE DEVELOPMENT PROCESS

The development of the city and the region may be described in three major periods of development:

The Beginnings to 1850. The period of Spanish/Mexican rule, the Rancho and Mission which began the transformation from a native agrarian culture to an urbanised society.

American Conquest, 1850s to 1900. The period of the Civil War, Mexican-American War, Gold Rush, Statehood, the building of the Transcontinental Railway and the resulting population and land boom of the 1880s.

20th Century Los Angeles. The period of maximum urbanisation beginning at the turn of the century, the explosive growth following World War II, establishing contemporary Los Angeles and Southern California.

Local development is closely linked with that of the south-western region of the United States, which evolved from the 19th-century struggle for control. In the course of that struggle, Mexican independence from Spain preceded the Mexican-American War, resulting in 1848 in the annexation of an area which included Texas, California, Arizona, New Mexico, Nevada, Utah and a portion of Colorado. California was admitted to the Union in 1850.

It is a surprising historical note that missions were an early development strategy. The missions were to become secular and were converted into civilian towns with an emancipated Indian population. Folklore romanticises the destruction of the Indian population. The beginning of private land ownership was established in the form of large ranchos. These early holdings continued to influence the pattern of development into the 20th century. The Irvine Ranch, located in the south-west of Los Angeles in Orange County, is an example of thousands of privately owned acres (90 000) that may be traced to the Spanish grant system. The area became the site of a new town during the 1960s.

A legacy of conflict exists between the Spanish-Mexican and Anglo-American cultures, dating from the period of conquest. The endearing term 'greaser' was a local reference to Mexicans and Indians who loaded the hides of cattle on to clipper ships. The term became a synonym for any dark-skinned person. True to periods of conquest, the 1850s were a time of violence at both the societal and individual levels.

Historians have noted that less than 200 years have elapsed between the founding of El Pueblo de Los Angeles and the emergence of a post-industrial city-region. The history of the period is one of intense organisation, innovation and growth. In fact, its structural process and form are substantially different from the concentric patterns of growth common to the classical and industrial cities of the 19th century. References to suburban growth, low density and sprawl based upon auto transportation are common descriptions. These are at best partial explanations for the structure of Los Angeles.

The pattern of growth is dominated by 100 district cities and communities spread over the 5 000 square mile area of the County, with Los Angeles as the major city having an area in excess of 500 square miles. The description of Los Angeles as a '... collection of Suburbs in search of a city' (Carey McWilliams) remains a most apt description.

This development pattern encompasses all of Southern California. Sociologists, economists, political scientists and historians have attempted to describe local development. Although the descriptions vary, the culture of

Southern California pivots around the political influence of the suburban communities. Outside of the central area, the cities tend to be bedroom communities providing housing and related commercial services. The model of development is a mix of the urban and suburban.

One of the most significant features of the historical development of the region is the specialised form of local government which has accommodated and supported rapid growth. This was especially true for the period of expansion linked to massive investment in water and power distribution. From 1901 to 1930, there were 44 incorporations in Los Angeles County. The California Aqueduct, Boulder (Hoover) Dam and the Feather River Water projects were milestones in the development of a regional water system.

A second factor was a form of metropolitan government called the 'Lakewood Plan', which quickly and easily solved the problem of the provision of municipal services by means of a contract between a community and the county of Los Angeles. The services available to the various communities by contract included a full array of services which previously would have been provided by the city or community. These included health services, police protection, street maintenance, fire protection, parks, recreation and libraries. The Lakewood Plan was so successful that 25 new cities were incorporated between 1956 and 1960. The post-war 'Contract City' became an important component of a metropolitan government which allowed for services to large geographic areas, characterised by a high degree of urbanisation but low population density.

The low density form is more easily understood as a housing preference than as the result of administrative and political power. The 'California Bungalow' remains the preferred housing type. It is only during the past decade (1960-1970) that a shift from the single-family home may be observed in Los Angeles. For the present, the bungalow is simply being modified as the 'Condo' (single family condominium ownership). The low density form of Los Angeles will apparently continue with incremental shifts to more intensive development through the turn of the century.

The theory which explains the local government and political system is descriptive and only partly explains how several hundred governmental components at the city, county, state and federal levels operate in a cohesive and efficient way. A useful generalisation is that the local governmental structure is a unique network that evolved in response to growth as the sustaining factor. The low cost of providing these services to a cluster of new communities formed since World War II cannot be overlooked.

Current population projections are summarised below:

	1970	1990
State of California	22 000 000	30 000 000
LA County	7 000 000	7 790 600
LA City	2 800 000	3 600 000

The pattern of urbanisation of the 5 000 square-mile metropolitan area (LA County) is characterised by three distinct zones: North Los Angeles County (Antelope Valley); San Gabriel and Santa Monica Mountains (Angeles National Forest); and coastal plains and communities. The latter makes up the built-up area which is approximately one-third of the total metropolitan area. Approximately 86% of the region's growth was recorded in the

coastal plains during the past decade. However, there is significant speculation as to the accuracy of population projections. The city planning department has reduced population projections from 5 million by the year 2000 (1968 report) to 3.6 million (1976 report), a modest increase of 8% in 20 years. These projections are linked to population growth through immigration and natural increases, as well as by a potential shift in the pattern of urbanisation. The latter would involve an increase in the population of the older communities.

A real factor in population growth that escapes accurate measure is the 'illegal alien' problem (referring to Mexican nationals) who are arriving in increasing numbers from northern Mexico. This is part of a larger phenomenon of rapid increase in the 'Latino' or Spanish-speaking population. The *Los Angeles Times* (February 1978) described a 'vast shift ... In LA ethnic make-up' referring to the post-war period since the 1950s. The Anglo population has dropped from 80% to less than 50% within city boundaries. The Spanish population is the fastest growing, having surpassed the Black population by 1970. Current projections indicate that the Spanish-Black composition represents 27.5% and 21.5%, respectively, of the 2.8 million total population. An important demographic footnote describes the estimate of 400 000 illegal aliens as 'very conservative'. The Asian population has also surged during the past decade with increasing numbers of Japanese, Chinese, Korean, and Polynesian residents. In the Los Angeles scheme of things, this translates into 'Little Tokyo', 'Chinatown', and 'Koreatown'.

Banham's notion of the four ecologies of Los Angeles is shorthand for describing the city. The ecological analogy requires further development in any attempt to understand the wide range of socio-economic conditions that exist within the city. The spectrum encompasses grinding poverty at one end and great affluence on the other. The network of a large number of separate but linked communities in addition to accommodating growth serves the purpose of socio-economic stratification. Simply stated, the high-income residents are attracted to the foothills and canyons, the middle class to the suburbs, and the low-income residents are restricted to the central city and the older communities.

A view of the city's social structure emerges from understanding that major economic activities remain clustered in the central area in close proximity to downtown Los Angeles. This pattern has been described as the CBD, the Grey area and the inner ring of communities. The scale of the area in Los Angeles exceeds 50 square miles, larger than the entire city of San Francisco. Within this area is the greatest diversity and concentration of activity. The suburban rings are supported by the resources of central Los Angeles and its poor minority populations. This function of the Central City has been minimised in studies of the city. Closely related to social and physical stratification is racial segregation within the suburban communities. They are essentially white enclaves, while the enclaves of the Central City are dominated by black and brown ghettos and barrios.

Development through the turn of the century will reflect the potential for development within the Central City. The pattern of 'gentrification' which has gained momentum in other major cities may become the major form of development in older communities, as the low density pattern simply becomes economically obsolete.

Ed Niles
SERVICING SYSTEMS

Even a wasteland can be made to bear fruit – by those with the will, the water and the wealth.

Rick Gore, *The Desert*

This statement, appropriate as it is today, did not always apply in the LA basin. Eighteen thousand years ago man enjoyed a relative abundance of water and a large inventory of forests and animal life. As the climatology of the basin changed when the last ice receded, the abundance of water within the lower basins diminished, plant and animal

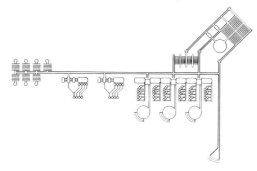

LA city map no 1 – 1849

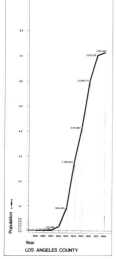

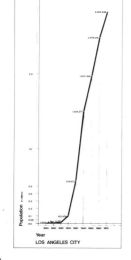

Population – millions

Year
LOS ANGELES COUNTY

Year
LOS ANGELES CITY

LA county population growth

life deteriorated, and man left the area in search of food and water. In the Spanish and early California mission period, the Los Angeles, San Gabriel and Santa Clara Rivers provided reliable access to water and subsurface wells. The Los Angeles River provided El Pueblo de los Angeles with its primary source of potable and agricultural water.

A series of events have formulated the present potable, industrial and agricultural water base of Los Angeles as we know it today. With the rapid growth of agriculture, especially of the citrus industry, traditional reserves of potable and irrigation waters from the hydrographic basins were quickly depleted. In 1880 the extension of the Southern Pacific Railroad, together with its commercial implications and aggressive land sales, initiated the first great land boom in the basin. The ensuing build-up of agricultural communities and institutions brought with it an increased need for water and power.

California is blessed if one knows how to take advantage of its resources. The blessing in 1907 was the great Sierra Nevada mountain range to the north. The snow melt from these mountains fed the Owens Valley and its rivers with a constant and predictable source of water throughout the year. The Los Angeles Owens River aqueduct was bonded and completed at the turn of the century.

The basin grew in political, demographic and agricultural terms, but its economic stature was still based upon agricultural pursuits. With the development of LA harbour in 1907, the produce of the Los Angeles, San Bernardino and Santa Clara regions began to move through the harbour and the Southern Pacific Railroad network. This reinforced Los Angeles as a commercially significant metropolitan area. Further growth in commercial and agricultural pursuits in the 1920s increased the consumption of water and initiated the search for other resources. To the east lay one of the largest and most spectacular river systems in the world, the Colorado River. Its power was to be harnessed with dams and hydro-electric stations, and later with a network of aqueducts, storage basins, power transmission stations and so on. This umbilical cord not only served Los Angeles but also brought agricultural realities to riverside county, Santa Ana and San Diego.

The formation of the metropolitan water district in 1928 united the major water purveyors in Southern California in an effort to secure and administrate water from the Colorado River. The Los Angeles Department of Water and Power was formed to administer and distribute water and power within the political boundaries of the city. Its primary source is still from the Owens Valley and mono basin with the next greatest percentage taken from the local ground water reservoirs. Supplementary needs are brought directly from the MWD.

The Second World War, and specifically the war in the Pacific, initiated the migration of population from the agricultural communities of California and middle America into the Los Angeles basin. Military training and related industries, such as the military aircraft industry, introduced these people to the climate and the 'California lifestyle'. By 1945, Middle America had found Southern California. Agricultural land in the San Fernando and San Gabriel Valleys was overrun with housing tracts, swimming pools, air-conditioners and laws. The consumption of water for agriculture was 25% of the demand for residential use. The impact of the population explosion generated institutional, commercial, industrial and residential structures. The net-

work of fire protection systems in the Los Angeles metropolitan and residential areas increased. The demand for greater flow capacity and for reconstruction of the existing network became urgent. The growth pains were not unique to Southern California alone. Growth in other metropolitan areas of California and increased demand for agricultural products throughout the world accelerated the search for a new source of water. The Sierra Nevadas once again provided this source of life. A thousand miles to the north the Feather River project was born. Hydro-electric facilities at Oroville Dam and Castaic reinforced the parallel need for energy in this growth period. Eventually, the project was to be called the California Aqueduct. Water brought with it the economic and social structure inherent in major cultures.

Southern California, historically, has been a predictable source of fossil fuels. Oil reserves, natural gas, and geothermal have been equal to the growth requirements of the basin in the past. The escalation of growth after the Second World War however increased the demand for fossil fuels beyond the immediate and national resources. The Department of Water and Power has sustained the basin with a combination of fossil fuel generating facilities, hydro-electric operations and, in the past twenty years, supplementary power from nuclear resources.

A primary energy and fossil fuel resource utilised within the metropolitan area is natural gas. The Los Angeles area, through the Southern California Gas Company, stores these reserves within large underground facilities under low pressure. The distribution system is a network under high pressure and distributes to the basin from Ventura Natural Gas fields and fields in Texas, with liquefied natural gas going through the port of San Pedro. The demand for natural or liquefied gas by industry within the basin has increased substantially over the past twenty years. Fossil fuels create conditions which deteriorate air quality, but natural gas does not foster high sulphur emissions, and its demand is therefore increased.

The immediate future for increased resources in the basin is dependent on two basic factors. The political activists of the 1960s and 1970s have identified areas of California which are defined as ecologically sensitive. These include the coastal plain, natural river and creek courses, and desert preserves. The second factor, which has immediate and possibly far-reaching implications, is the public reaction against nuclear generating stations. Given the status of these decisions, the future resources for water will have to come from reclamation, desalination and expensive northwest water linkages. California will be forced to limit its water demand from the Colorado River system by federal decree.

The development of alternative sources to nuclear energy seems more promising. Extensive geothermal in the imperial valley and the development of the California power pool tied to dams on the Columbia River systems constitute at present a practical solution to growth until the year 2000. The coal-fired steam turbine generators at Four Corners, New Mexico are only the beginning in a possible network of coal-related energy production. All of this energy will be produced out of state because of the environmental decisions made. The spectre of limiting the growth of these generating facilities by future environmental laws within Arizona and New Mexico must not however be ignored.

The future lies in the internal solution of water resources and energy within California.

Roberts Dam

Water supply pipes

Power lines

Nuclear power plant

Water supply

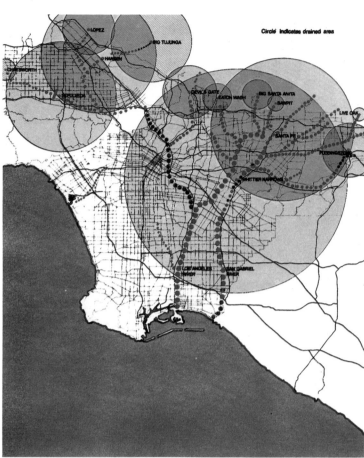

Flood control

The opening of the LA Aqueduct

One of LA's reservoirs

Power supply

Frank Dimster
CHARACTER OF THE METROPOLIS

Section through LA

SANTA CATALINA ISLAND SAN PEDRO BASIN PALOS VERDES DOWNTOWN SAN GABRIEL MOUNTAINS MOJAVE DESERT

Coastal California Coastal Sage Southern Oak Coastal Sagebrush Southern Chaparral Mixed Ponderosa/ Joshua Oak Hardwood Jeffrey Pine Tree Mojave Creosote Bush adapted from ATLAS of CALIFORNIA

Ventura Boulevard 1922

East on Wilshire at Hauser

Two major issues coincided in Los Angeles to reinforce each other, and as a result played a dominant role in the development of the region. The classical urban form with which we are familiar (and to which we are often very attached) provides a dense concentration of people and facilities around a central core of a civic and community character. This classical pattern was questioned and replaced in Los Angeles as the ideal form of settlement for a post-industrial society where value systems had been altered, the definitions of economy and productivity had been changed, and one had the potential of a vast national transportation and communication network; both of these possible organising systems were decentralised as to control and ownership, miniaturised by technology, and had the capacity of an extreme degree of sophistication as well as demand-response.

This condition offered a substantial amount of attraction due to the general disenchantment of the population with big government, its inefficiencies, and the rise in importance of regional and local issues. The decentralisation of governmental concerns and their focus was eventually taken up by the respective local governments.

It is important at this point to mention that the idea of decentralisation had and still has a very special appeal to the American — it is an attraction that has been traditionally celebrated in every form of communication: it represents a reduced risk of totalitarian government control.

Such a decentralised urban organisation, of which we are part in Los Angeles, has other and possibly more quantifiable advantages in terms of resource utilisation of the country as a whole and the necessary infrastructure networks to provide the lifestyles everyone has been taught both to pursue and to attain. It is certainly for these reasons, among others, that the National Resource Planning Board in 1935 recommended ways to encourage industrial and related residential decentralisation in the countryside.

In this context, Los Angeles represented a lifestyle for the adventurous. It offered an increased degree of personal freedom from all aspects. These options were realised in job opportunities and lifestyle environments so that one could simulate on a miniature scale the public definition of 'grand' living. Hollywood provided the imagery, the city, the jobs, and a varied topography and mild climate.

Thus, here in Los Angeles, the notion of self-sufficiency

LAPD surveillance

Animal cemetery

Downtown parking

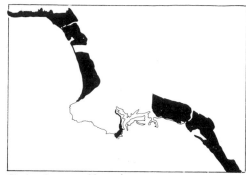

expressed by John Ruskin and Ralph Borsodi became a tangible reality for many people who had experienced disappointment elsewhere. The motivations and certainly the expectations of various waves of new urban settlers to the Los Angeles region are complex, although there is a well-rooted belief in America which envisions a culture without cities. Emerson, Thoreau, and Whitman are very articulate spokesmen for this point of view. The cities are seen as a place of social immorality and political corruption, a major contrast to the classical, perhaps European, counterpart which celebrates the city as a place of intellectual leadership, culture, and social refinement.

Thus, the Los Angeles form of alternative has only very recently been acknowledged by the architectural and urban planning professions. The phenomenal growth and public acceptance of the suburbs, the small towns, and the relatively low densities which characterise the automobile-orientated cities are part of a continuous urbanisation process rather than a regressive and misdirected orientation. These dispersed communities had to depend heavily on major developments in transportation of all modes and the necessary communication networks to support both.

The technologies which made these urban alternatives possible as well as desirable helped in defining a new expression of a uniquely American lifestyle, one which hoped to find a viable balance between the collective benefits of a classical urban order and self-sufficiency of the individual in control of his future, between urbanism and agrarianism, between historically influenced models and a response to demands for personal comforts and choice: this is the principal order and attraction of Los Angeles, in addition to the God-given assets mentioned before. This vast and amorphous suburb, lacking any dominant physical order and featuring extremely large horizontal dimensions, is not what one expected a major city housing millions to look like.

The perception of LA as contradictory and esoteric in nature was most commonly experienced by professionals as a result of their preconceived notions of the 5000 year-old classic city model. The gap between expectation and reality was the root cause of endless ridicule and criticism about Los Angeles.

This new order represented by Los Angeles and other automobile-orientated cities of a smaller size, such as

Houston or Phoenix, has had a much shorter history than its classical counterpart, particularly since the disciplines of planning and architecture are very closely tied to the history and development of the traditional city model.

Only a handful of professionals, however, have accepted these patterns, studied them, and developed new concepts of urbanisation. It is perhaps not surprising that Great Britain provided the earliest, most articulate, and energetic leadership in this regard in spokesmen like Reyner Banham, Archigram, Derek Walker and Cedric Price, while Robert Venturi and Denise Scott Brown represent possibly the most consciously sympathetic domestic viewpoint.

The yearning for freedom is a peculiarly American theme which recurs periodically in American folklore ranging from Walt Whitman to the most current and popular television stories and songs that use the open road as a metaphor. In this context, the individual automobile is the equalising vehicle in social and often economic terms. Even the most dismal areas in the city can be escaped to enjoy the beach, the parks, or the manicured residential streets of the wealthiest districts. Thus, the automobile, the symbol of freedom and choice, can both transport and distribute resources as well as provide nightmare difficulties for law enforcers. It is this condition which made the professional planners, investors, and politicians use the transportation network as the primary element to structure all planning activities.

This transportation system, as others which dominated before the automobile, also created a pattern of accessibility which in turn dictated land-use distribution and the related land values and densities. As a result of these developments, transportation planning gained the dominant role in the planning profession it enjoyed in the Sixties. The fall-out effect can be seen in architecture, where circulation moved up in the organisational and expressive concerns of many projects.

Evidence of the new focus on movement during this period is the 1962 Highway Act, which for the first time made large sums of federal money available to the cities. Partially as a result of this Act, cities such as Los Angeles found themselves in a period of rapid development underpinned by an equally rapid evolution of sophisticated planning techniques for forecasting, modelling, data assimilation and data processing. Thus, the future order,

expansion, and functioning of both urban and suburban areas were determined by armed professionals whose scientific methods were designed to replace intuitive, aesthetic, formalistic, and often irrational approaches formerly identified with architecture. In this way, planners moved into a new era of rational decision- making·

It was hoped that this attitude would spill over into other disciplines; however, this did not occur. No one anticipated the public backlash to the highway and freeway programme, nor did they expect the appearance of environmental protection and reconstruction as a major political issue. Thus, the exclusion of politics in these rationalists' models, the oil crisis, and the emergence of minorities as a political power (particularly in urban areas where the remaining pieces of the transportation system were to be built) all caused a serious re-examination of the dominant priorities. The revitalisation of urban mass transit systems gained new attention and some spotty popular support. This period of re-evaluation can be observed in Los Angeles: it is possibly a typical sequence of events in other cities and it draws attention to the refinement and better use of existing facilities, right-of-way networks, and equipment hardware. Since this is a very young city, the overlapping layers of transportation networks and modes are still clearly evident; the experiment to test and find alternatives is easier here.

Los Angeles is the built prototype of a new social order, the order of a pluralistic value system and the rapidly changing proximities of a mosaic society. We have to look, however briefly, at one very important element in this new order: the streets of Los Angeles. The system of major arterials and freeways make it possible for this large metropolis to function, and function rather well. Here we find a cohesive network of public spaces, a continuous system providing all services, such as aid in the event of fires, riot, crime, accidents, etc. The same system provides the vehicle for the dislocated and disadvantaged to seek opportunities elsewhere, as mentioned before. It is here in the street where many of the social dramas unfold, to relieve the concerned and to inform the isolated.

For the four million registered automobile owners of the city within an area of almost 500 square miles, such an urban organisation is perceived and understood by residents in a different way. The public spaces of the streets and boulevards dominate one's experience in the

Beach picnic

Beach at Santa Monica

Beach edge

LA mountainous areas

city and form the spatial pattern we remember. The architectural composition lining the steets is secondary and in fact often hidden by vegetation. Thus, the identity of an area is given by the dominant street use and not by dominant buildings. These activities can occur at different times and for both institutional and spontaneous reasons.

The expression of the need for individual freedom and identity balanced with the collective benefits of urban congregations, the coexistence of the cities with intellectual and cultural leadership and the cherished values of the countryside can be found in Los Angeles. It is a very comfortable city in which to live and a very difficult city to visit. This city is a quilt of miniatures which are often the built recollections of the various waves of new residents.

So it can be seen that midwestern types prevail in Santa Monica, while the opposition lives in Venice, and those with some hope of self-sufficiency in Topanga Canyon. It is quite possible that the post-industrial city has found its form in Los Angeles as classical cities found their expression at different times. The success of this form is dependent on the validity of our individual value system and the appropriate role of our institutions. It is a city without cathedrals and palaces, without formal gardens or physical fortifications; it will have to be a city with conviction and determination resulting from the strength which is an aggregate of its parts. The experiment here will have to show if our mosaic society can describe an overall desirable image within the language of our society and not that of an outmoded classical expression.

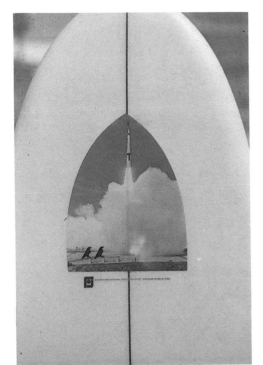

Surf cult

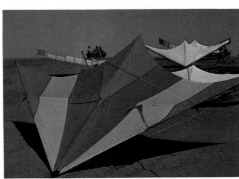

Hang gliding

Lotus

Marina

City grain

Diagram – principal geographical features

Pasadena City Hall

Scale variety

Hotel Green Pasadena

Belair

Car cult

Freeway planting

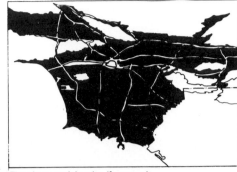

The pieces and the glue 'freeways'

Sepulveda

Bungalow style

Breakfast at the Beverly Hills Hotel

Echo Park

Billboard signing

Street scene

Diagram of man-made and natural condition

Sunset at Santa Monica

San Bernardino Town Hall

Public transport Wilshire corridor

Swap mart

View over the city

33

Emmet L Wemple
THE LANDSCAPE SALAD

Californian poppies

The Los Angeles landscape today gives little evidence of the original form and character of the land except in parts of the Santa Monica and San Gabriel Mountains. It is here that one can still see the land as it was 200 years ago, and such places become the only source of study of native plant and animal communities, providing the last remaining image of the area before various immigrations The Los Angeles basin and foothills have been eroded by the technology of earth movers, covered with asphalt and concrete and a diverse array of architectural form, and then decorated with plants introduced from nearly every part of the world. Each newcomer has brought plants and styles that fulfilled a nostalgia for home; now, nearly 95 per cent of our ornamental plants are strangers. Australia, Asia, South Africa and Europe are well represented and have been with us so long that species like the Eucalypti are thought by many to be indigenous. Nurseryman Theodore Payne was one who sought to protect and propagate native plants and endeavoured to encourage appreciation for the subtle beauty and unusual character of the wild lilac, toyon, poppy, lupine and oak among many others. Landscape architects Edward Huntsman-Trout and Ralph Cornell were thoughtful and insistent about the manner in which new plantings were used in this arid region; Huntsman-Trout frowned on and resisted the use of carpets of lawn grass as he considered them inappropriate and far too demanding of precious water.

From the earliest time the growth and development of the land was dependent on water, and the meager sources deterred many until calculated efforts (based on greed, ambition and political prowess) brought water from the Owens Valley in 1913. Two hundred-and-fifty miles of aqueduct and engineering skill supplied the region and made possible the rash development of the San Fernando Valley. Later still, the renowned feat of diverting more from the Colorado River gave Los Angeles the additional resource for growth and change.

To fully appreciate all of this, I would recommend that those interested in learning go into the California 'wilderness' without water and spend a day wandering through the fields and hills in mid-August. With good fortune, one might fine one of the small streams with a trickle of water supplied from the winter rains among the golden brown hills and, perhaps, enjoy the shade of the sycamore at the stream's edge or the live oak on a nearby slope.

Los Angeles and environs were coveted from the beginning, due in part to the gentle climate and the potential opportunities of a new land. The occasional earthquakes led to a disquieting notion about its future, but the promise of gold or riches from land speculation overshadowed doubt, and people from Europe and the eastern United States joined the established Mexican population in their desires for success and opportunity. Still others arrived with the discovery of oil in 1904 and, as in the Gold Rush, few became rich but many remained to add to the growing population. In the late 1800s, others hoping to enjoy the benefits of the warm sun and promises of renewed health, arrived by ship, transcontinental stage and, later, the newly founded Pacific Railroad. For 30 years, they came and burdened the city; there was neither adequate housing nor ample water for so many.

At the same time, promoters and commercial zealots sent coloured picture postcards to the east, depicting large mansions surrounded by flowering vines and shrubs and captioned: 'A typical California cottage in mid-winter'. An advertising programme sponsored by the newly organised Sunkist Growers campaigned in the mid-west with the slogan 'Oranges for Health, California for Wealth'. The Depression and great drought in the central, southern United States provided a hardy and determined influx of people who added much to the heterogenous mix of immigrants. Not until the end of World War II was there another significant surge of new arrivals, the young veterans who came in the late 1940s. They had experienced Los Angeles on their way to war, recalling on their return to the middle and eastern United States, the soft winters and receptive spirit of the place and its people, and returned to raise their families.

Where else could one drive in a private automobile and in an eight-hour period experience the beach and ocean of Santa Monica, the sage-covered foothills, the high desert and Josua trees, and then ski on pine-covered mountain slopes? Freedom of choice was the great virtue, coupled with a land that offered so much and resisted so little.

Perhaps the best examples of landscape architecture are to be found in the residential gardens, where a new form developed. The original larger gardens of the wealthy emulated Europe and the eastern seaboard estates, and never really expressed or responded well to the land and climate. By trial, need and recognition of the opportunity, architecture and garden became extensions of each other. Even today, one can see Angelenos enthusiastically transporting plants from place to place in the back of their vans, autos and pick-up trucks, and avidly reading Sunset books and the various 'How to Do It' books published in the west.

The freeways, born in Southern California, were another unique and important contribution, not only for their architectural forms but also for the manner in which their edges, interchanges and slopes are treated. Concrete ribbons divide the city into chunks as they weave and undulate; at times, they appear in man-made valleys, then rise above and provide unusual and dramatic views of the city. The plantings provide a varied arboretum at every turn and pocket of inaccessible space.

The two major urban parks totalling 4683 acres are Elysian Park and Griffith Park. As part of the city, they provide a rare potential of open space, but only with extreme care and judicious planning will they become significant as part of the urban structure. One can only hope that they be allowed simply to exist until proper and careful planning is available, before they are misused by poor development or impatient and naive ambitions. These and other parks have been preserved by anxious and concerned citizens who have a greater sense of civic horizons than the administrators responsible for them. Without citizen concern and demands, open spaces would be filled with convention centers, oil exploration and more stadiums like the Dodger Stadium.

Urban spaces in the form of plazas, courts and streets are mere tokens to what they might be. The city streets respond primarily to the automobile as they should but are no more than paved paths for the pedestrian. Both public and private courts, plazas and malls do not respond well to the needs of the people they are meant to serve, and they seem to be only poor copies of other places. Most are furnished with 'shelf items' from various manufacturers with little thought to scale or compatibility. The Security Pacific complex tries to provide all things for all people and is successful in its redundancy. Arco Plaza takes its role seriously and is what it was meant to be, a severe, symbolic gesture to sophisticated bankers and clerks. Most unfortunate are the series of spaces called the Civil Center Mall, which begins with a sculpture by Lipschitz and ends with the grotesque triforium and a jumble of light standards, benches and confused paving patterns. One must walk down Broadway or Seventh Street or visit Olvera Street on a Sunday to learn how people respond to each other and to the spaces they are in.

Los Angeles is fortunate, for in many ways it is not too late. Bunker Hills and the City Center are still under development and salvation may not be in what is built but rather in where it is built and what is left. That which is left, left alone or touched with gentle but firm hands will be the landscape. The open space, like the white space on the printed page, is critical, for it takes vision, maturity and sense to appreciate its value.

There is little time to write about it, seminar it, lecture it or case-study it — only time enough to be dedicated and creative and sensitive to one, if not the last, western frontier.

High Palm Street looking East

Typical street foliage

Desert landscape

Freeway planting

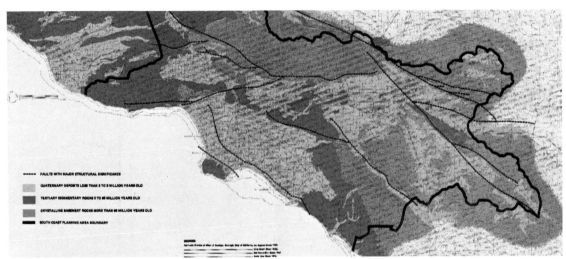
Geological formations

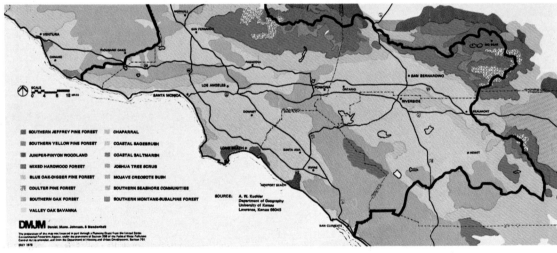
Historic native plant communities

Areas of ecological significance

Diagrams: the Southern Californian Association of Governments

Coastal mist

Santa Monica Pier

Laguna

Marina

Santa Monica

Desert plants

Mount Ensenada

Thorn

San Bernardino Mountains

Kelp

Santa Monica

Moonstone Beach

Balboa

Refugio Pass

Santa Monica landscape

Freeway downtown LA

Hispanic Manicure SM

Forest San Bernardino

Beverly Hills

Forest Lawn

Beverly Hills

Beverly Glen

Bel Air

Desert road

San Bernardino Mountains

Mojave Desert pear

Meadow Farm

Desert plants

Old gold mine

Mojave Desert

Relics of forest fire

Red Rock Canyon, Mojave

Mojave landscape

JOHN NICOLAIS, 1940–1979

Paradise Ballroom LA

California oranges

Street scene LA

Puppets, Olvera Street

One of the more positive reasons that made this issue possible was the photographic collection that John Nicolais had assembled quietly and methodically over the last 15 years of changing Los Angeles. It provided the visual fuel and lubrication for almost all the contributors. It was a delight to the eye and a thoughtful record of most aspects of Los Angeles life and architecture.

John's tragic battle with Hodgkin's disease ended in October 1979, when he died at the Cedars of Sinai Hospital in Los Angeles. His death at 39 was a tragic loss to an architectural community who loved him as a gentle, talented architect, artist and photographer. His exquisite taste and uncanny knack for capturing the essence of every subject he photographed, however trivial or banal, put him firmly in the dynasty of great architectural photographers. In a city that has produced such marvellous photographers as Marvin Rand and Julius Schulman, this assessment has real meaning. The tragedy of his early death deprives us of an eye that combined wit, perception and candour.

Though much too ill to participate in the final photographic selection for this issue, John did the first rough editing with me in autumn 1978 from a collection of over 20,000 slides. His knowledge of the city was encyclopaedic, and possessing the great capacity of any good teacher, he left one continually elated, on tenterhooks for the next tray of visually stimulating and inevitably revealing photographic comments on the environment.

His crippling illness made his architectural life difficult in latter years. His allegiance to architecture was total and his promising early years as a student at the University of Philadelphia, in the office at GBQC Philadelphia and his years with Doshi, his great friend at the School of Architecture in Ahmedabad, India, underlined his two outstanding qualities – a continuous commitment to quality and an overwhelming sympathy for the underprivileged. His photographic journeys through India and Nepal betray these principles in every frame.

The loss of a richly gifted person early in life is a tragedy in terms of what might have been. The compensation for those who knew John is that his nature and his talent are recorded in his photographs. He died in the midst of a close-knit and loving family, his dignity and compassion undiminished. I was privileged to have known him and to have counted myself his friend. It is with great pleasure that I speak for all my friends and colleagues at the University of Southern California in dedicating our work in this issue to him.

Derek Walker

Beach, Santa Monica

Ocean in June

Ali Baba's

Art deco LA

40

Christian message

Free wheeling

Pediment LA

Ladies of LA

LA party

Quiet times

Downtown at Dusk

Pacific Sunset

Twin palms

Shopping on Rodeo

Pocket dog

It's in your head

41

2. THE ARCHITECTURE OF LOS ANGELES

Bradbury Building entrance, downtown LA

Alson Clark

INTRODUCTION

The fact that LA will celebrate its 200th birthday in 1981 has caused little stir among the populace, as almost everyone realises that this is a 'paper' anniversary. For 75 years, LA was a seedy back-water Pueblo on the fringes of the Spanish Empire, and for 35 more it was a small Victorian place filled with pattern-book mediocrities. In fact we don't like to think we're growing old at all. When the Beaux-Arts LA Public Library and Pasadena City Hall began to acquire a patina which might have mellowed them, cosmetic spray-painters were rushed to the scene, in the former case destroying the subtle distinction between the plaster walls and the stone relief panels which Bertram Goodhue and Lee Lawrie, his sculptor-collaborator, had so carefully planned. Never mind: another wrinkle had been hidden.

We are young and determined to stay that way. We are also quite rich, at least wealthy enough to re-landscape the whole of our recently acquired property. We found it much too drab, so most of the arid Colorado Desert has been converted into green golf environments, where ex-Presidents can get in 18 holes every single day, because it never rains. For the masses there is the landscape of the freeways. Miles of eucalyptus and acacia (not native plants) blot out the tacky development of the valleys, suggesting that these semi-deserts are some kind of 'Arcadias'. All this has attracted people who find their tradition-bound native heaths stultifying and regard LA as a relief if not an escape.

It was not always so, at least not so much so. When we began to get rolling decisions had to be made. Decisions used to be made by the rich and powerful, and Henry Edwards Huntington arrived rich and powerful and decided to build a transit system which would link the whole vast place together. Of course this set the pattern of sprawl which is our most distinctive characteristic. After the lines were built in record time, Huntington decided LA needed some roots. As time went on he had to be dissuaded from buying every First Folio Shakespeare and Romney portrait he could lay his hands on, in order that something might be left over to endow the cultural complex he was building in his princely park. There was the question of style for the buildings at 'San Marino Ranch'. He rather liked the one-storey wooden houses (bungalows) that were springing up in Huntington Park, Huntington Beach and all the other hamlets along his routes. He liked the more elaborate versions eastern millionaires were building as winter cottages in Pasadena, the town adjoining the Huntington holdings; he even had a large 'Craftsman' run up for his son. But wood is not terribly permanent, so in 1908, he employed Myron Hunt, a well-trained, well-travelled architect, to build a place with white plaster walls, red-tiled hipped roofs and cut-back, refined cornices and pediments. American Beaux-Arts was then known in Europe as 'chaste', a term which architectural critics no longer seem to employ.

The Mediterranean 'roots' approach seemed to be the thing. White walls and red-tiled roofs were to tie together the monumental Civic Center which was planned in 1922 for the heart of 'old' LA. Actually only one such building was completed. Roots did best when architects had something to relate to. Santa Barbara, a charming little spot up the coast, actually *had* a Mission and some *real* old houses, and James Osborne Craig and George Washington Smith went on from there to create the most convincing Mediterranean oeuvre of the region. It is significant that the University of California, Santa Barbara, has the only systematic collection of documents relating to the area's architectural past. No one in LA thought they were particularly interesting.

There was a shortage of true relics, and most of those were anything but romantic. To please the folks who loved to ride the 'Pacific Electric', Henry Huntington financed the Mission Inn. It grew over the years into a marvellous example of what people thought the Spaniards ought to have built, had they been a little more enterprising. It is the most significant monument of the 'Day-dream' style.

The palms, oranges and eucalyptus were soon thriving and the population was growing equally fast. Younger Beaux-Arts trained architects sensed the uniqueness of LA and wanted to express it. The bounds of the city were still somewhat under control, so the many groups of buildings which people like Stiles Clements built around Western Avenue gave LA a sense of place for the moment. The patterns of the form boards gave the concrete commercial structures scale; the large areas of steel sash, often arranged as rows of simple verticals, lighted the interiors well. Churriguerresque or Mayan ornament emphasised and enlivened the more important parts. The residential work of Wallace Neff combined simple Andalusian forms with dove-cote towers, topped by weathervanes in the shape of galleons. A Neff plan, admittedly atypical, was the Villa Papa Gulia, turned around backwards so that autos could sweep up. Inside it was the Villa Rotunda, but in this case the circular central space was an ellipse. Arthur Zwebell and others translated this approach into multi-family complexes around courts, and the builders made whole districts coherent with less inspired versions.

After the Twenties, the coherent shape of LA was destroyed. All the flat areas had been plotted in gigantic gridirons, one road so many hundred feet wide per mile, one a little narrower per half mile, and so on. Presumably, this was to take care of traffic problems for all time. Place gave way to circulation. All the hamlets began to be joined together to form the present city.

The Depression struck and brought what was thought to be an end to the eclectic era. Actually it had been building up for some time. In 1923 Alice Millard, a Huntington employee in the book-collecting department, built a house in Pasadena. It is uncertain whether the aged Henry Huntington ever visited 'La Miniatura', but if he did he probably didn't like it. Motives borrowed from savages were not likely to bring culture to his domain. Schindler had come, caught the spirit, and built his little masterpieces almost unnoticed. Neutra, more conscious of critics, had his first real commission, the 'Health House', included in the famous MOMA 'Modern Architecture' show of 1932. There were admonitions from Hitchcock and Johnson about not being pure enough. They must never have visited LA! Of course nothing by Schindler was considered pure enough for the show, which visited LA. It was housed, not in a museum, but at Bullock's Wilshire, now the best remaining example of the moderne era. Architecture is hardly some-thing that belongs in a museum here. Bullock's Wilshire is one of the few major modern buildings not threatened with destruction. Our vigilant, intelligent preservationists are fighting to save the others. Preservation may seem a strange activity for LA, but saving things like the Schindler House with government help is an activity which has solid local support.

The product of the sober, rational years of the Depression escapes the notice of visitors because it is so self-effacing. The work of Harwell Harris, Gregory Ain and other architects and builders were meant to serve the needs of the people who built them. You have to get out and walk to see them, and few hurried visitors bother to do that, when they can have such fun hunting down giant dough-nuts.

Arts and Architecture, which documented this era and the time of the Case Study houses which followed, is no longer published. At times it seems as if we hardly know what's going on unless we drive around or look at pictures in undecipherable Japanese magazines. The corporate packages we see in *A plus U* seem to be more interesting than their Miesian counterparts of the Sixties, and of course Cesar Pelli's Design Centre, although not as pure as the work of the New York Five (this is LA), is the source of some local pride. Charles Moore, who defies classification (he is already an Angelino) has built a few things, and everyone looks forward to more.

Oldenburg is now hung in the same museums as Poussin, so our whole crazy city has become an art form. It has spread to about its limits and what is happening now is infill. In the older districts this kind of thing, when done well, seems to pull things together. A little pink plaster High Tech (or is it Low Tech?) duplex by Gehry or someone like that set down in a Venice street of old vernacular is something that has not occurred much in LA, where vast areas were developed all at once. Our latest leap forward has been encouraged, if not made possible, by the establishment of two new centres of architectural thought, UCLA and SCI-Arch. These have encouraged the older schools to become more stimulating.

We sometimes wish H E Huntington could be reincarnated and would proceed to give us a transit system in jig time. The proposed substitute has been floundering through the democratic process for nearly 20 years and, since the oil derricks on Signal Hill stopped pumping, this has given us an uneasy feeling. We have reached the age when we are reviving our revivals, but this should not be taken as a sign of old age if you examine the product closely. It is not nearly as good as the Twenties, as nobody really bothered to learn any lessons from the rich work of that period all over town.

We are rediscovering our modern tradition. We discovered Schindler, rediscovered Schindler, and are now re-rediscovering Schindler. But it seems to do no harm. There are no Schindler revival buildings to speak of. We are producing beautiful drawings of the old and the new by the carload, now that we have a good educational set-up. It's about time for this, and some of them are bound to be built. It was said at least 40 years ago that LA was 25 suburbs in search of a city. This still fits, but at least the suburbs are growing more interesting.

THE BRADBURY BUILDING

Lift and roof detail

Lift detail

Fire equipment

General view

Lift gear

Newel post

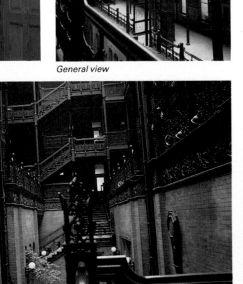

Parallel view

Staircase well

View to lower hall

Balcony detail

Detail wrought iron

Landing detail

Mayan Theatre detail

K Paul Zygas
THE ECLECTIC TRADITION

Los Angeles is commonly thought to have more than a fair share of curious, bizarre, and entertaining buildings. But this is only a popular illusion, a mental image widespread among Los Angelenos and visitors alike. Actually, most of LA is carpeted mile after mile by undistinguished frame and stucco constructions forming a neutral visual field that is neither perceived nor remembered. Given this backdrop, even a mildly unconventional intrusion causes more visual impact and becomes more memorable than would otherwise be reasonable to expect. Furthermore, Southern California's topography and climate as well as its social and economic history have all conspired to reinforce the impression that LA is a city of impermanent and theatrical special effects.

The terrain underlying LA's thin, man-made veneer is for the most part also monotonous and featureless. Except for the diminutive La Brea tar pits, no other natural landmark distinguishes or articulates metropolitan LA's 1200 square-kilometer basin, which is framed by the Pacific Ocean on the west and south and the Santa Monica and San Gabriel mountains on the north. And as for LA's river, it's a joke. A strolling visitor once remarked: 'I fell into the Los Angeles river and almost drowned in the dust.'

Low hills modulate the surface of LA's basin and their presence has affected sections of the city's street layout. But for quick orientation, local topographic details should be ignored so that the entire metropolis may be viewed as a gridiron which is aligned to the cardinal points of a compass. Though the grid layout covers LA very effectively as a neutralising device, certain streets and certain sections of the city are readily identifiable as urban set-pieces with an established nomenclature and a well-known, historically sanctioned genealogy.

Wilshire Boulevard, for instance, LA's principal east-west artery, is equivalent to the Roman *decumanus*. Figueroa Street, running north-south, represents the *cardo*. Appropriately enough, their intersection locates a nearby forum – Pershing Square, which is surrounded by the thick concentration of public, commercial, and cultural institutions of the downtown area. A few blocks to the north, we find an *acropolis*. Once defended by Fort Moore, the high ground is presently the setting for the Civic Center and W Beckett's Music Center – appropriately nicknamed the 'Parthenon of the West'. On the eastern slope Olivera Street functions as the resuscitated, pre-Roman *agora*. And a few paces more to the east, the majestic Union Passenger Terminal symbolises a triumphal arch hailing all those fortunate enough to arrive in or leave LA by rail.

On returning to the *cardo/decumanus* intersection and proceeding northwards on Figueroa St, J Portman's Bonaventure Hotel is too obvious to be missed. Further along in the same direction we would pass Dodger Stadium and arrive in Pasadena where the Rose Bowl, the Gamble House, F L Wright's Millard House, and the Jet Propulsion Laboratory are all located in the vicinity of Figueroa Street's northern termination. Altogether this street runs more than 40 kilometres. Its southern end reaches San Pedro, site of the cute Ports O'Call village, the ferry terminal to Catalina Island, and the Los Angeles Harbor. The 'landmark' Queen Mary is moored a few miles eastward, while Marineland and Lloyd Wright's Wayfarer's Chapel lie several miles west of San Pedro.

The *documanus* of 'Miracle Mile' fame, Wilshire Boulevard, stretches some 25 kilometres from downtown LA to the beaches of the Pacific Ocean. Proceeding westward from its intersection with Figueroa Street, we would sequentially encounter these landmarks: the Granada Building, Bullock's Wilshire Department Store, the Wiltern Theatre, the Rancho La Brea Tar Pits, and the LA Country Museum of Art. The Boulevard continues through Beverley Hills before descending to the Pacific Coast Highway before descending to the Pacific Coast Highway which takes us to Malibu and the famous (infamous to some) J Paul Getty Museum.

Despite the clarity of the gridiron and despite the prominence of the urban set-pieces in LA's downtown, neither coalesces in our minds as a memorable *Gestalt*. By contrast, visitors to LA most often remember its freeways, either with admiration or disgust. And for better or worse, it is the freeways (rather than individual buildings, or grand avenues, or public spaces) that remain ineradicably associated with Los Angeles. Because the freeways create the total LA context and because they condition the perception of LA's architecture, eclectic or not, we must give the freeways their due.

Ironically, and imperceptible to the visitor's eye, LA's freeway system reinforces the underlying grid-iron street network. The Harbor/Pasadena Freeway, for instance, runs parallel to Figueroa St and therefore functions as a high-speed *cardo*. Seen in this way, Santa Monica Freeway, which parallels Wilshire Blvd, becommes a *decumanus* reincarnated as a superhighway. Downtown buildings terminate Wilshire Blvd, but the Santa Monica continues eastward relentlessly as the Pomona Freeway. The two freeway pairs are continuous highways, only their names change when they pass the downtown intersection in their respective north/south and east/west directions. As for orientation, most freeway drivers will locate their destination points within the quadrants sectioned off by the Harbor/Pasadena *cardo* and the Santa Monica/Pomona *decumanus*.

On locating the destination within its quadrant, the driver will use the most appropriate combination of radial and circumferential highways to reach his or her goal. Since the radial and circumferential highway network crisscrosses the surface street gridiron as well as the superhighway *cardo/decummanus* mentioned above, orientation and access in LA is only a relatively minor irritant. However, the journey itself and its after-effects are quite another matter. Because of the distances involved, driving in LA is extremely time-consuming. Pasadena and San Pedro, for example, are separated by about an hour (two-hour round trip) on the continuous Pasadena/Harbor Freeway, if one drives at 80 kilometers per hour (50 mph); at the same speed, half an hour is needed on the Santa Monica Freeway to reach the beaches nearest to downtown LA. In general, trips within the LA basin require about a half hour on average, plus a safety margin for unexpected delays in congested traffic.

Unlike 30-minute trips on London's womb-like Tube, even shorter trips on LA's freeways deaden the senses and dull the perceptions because the concentration required for high-speed driving requires a suspension of normal sense perception. Add to this the psycho-logical demands made by driving in dry, hot weather, frequently during the jam-ups of the rush hour, and constantly with the glare of the sun affecting the field of vision in one way or another. The cumulative effect debilitates.

With the senses deadened by a long car ride, familiar objects coming into view provide genuine relief. And the more familiar the object, the better. Hence the popularity and memorability of hot-dog stands looking like hot-dogs, ice-cream stands built as inverted ice-cream cones, shop-fronts of photography stores resembling enlarged cameras, and short-order restaurants inviting you to lay down your hat. The familiar object that is enlarged to architectural scale need not even bear a direct relationship to the activities that it encloses. In fact, the associational relation may be irrelevant, or tenuous (Coca-Cola Bottling Plant = Atlantic liner; Samson Tire Co. = walls of Babylon). The imagery may even be stretched to break all the usual mental links. But as long as the image is familiar, weary drivers will recognise and remember it as a landmark too blatant and outrageous to be missed or forgotten.

Conventional architecture this is certainly not, but as advertising these images do very well: the eye has been caught, the attention sustained, the company and its product remembered. Moreover, the enlarged ice-cream cones, hot dogs, and derby hats function as three-dimensional billboards into which we may enter and move about. But never mind looking for architectural sequences or spatial manipulations; they are not to be found in the horse-laundry behind the paper-maché palomino or in a steak house under a wire-and-stucco Angus bull.

As for architecture proper, ie buildings which advertise nothing but their own design, we should bear in mind that the characteristic development during the 19th and 20th centuries was one of ever-changing styles, the brave aspirations of modern architecture included. It should therefore come as no surprise that the buildings of a 200 year-old city, such as Los Angeles, reflect the design kaleidoscope of the times plus a few local variations on the international themes.

Consequently, a surprising selection from the stylistic cornucopia of the last century may still be encountered in Los Angeles and Southern California. Admittedly, most of the styles appeared in late and diluted form: Greek Revival transformed into the Monterey Style, English Arts & Crafts transformed into the Craftsman Style. Others, such as the Gothic Revival appeared here in various guises: Carpenter's Gothic, Eastlake, Stick Style. But none of these stylistic artifices were local inventions; all of them had been imported from the East or from Europe, and throughout the English-speaking world all were received in their day as the admired norm.

With periodic building booms afflicting the area from the 1800s to the present, LAs architecture reflects with a vengeance the international design milieu. The speculative builders of each successive wave had few ambitions as designers. Instead, they were immensely satisfied to construct pleasing reproduction of the architecture that the *nouveau riche* were commissioning throughout the civilised world. As a result, good examples of Queen Anne and excellent examples of Colonial Revival are relatively abundant throughout the city's older sections. And if the client aspired to status untainted by Anglophilia, local architects and builders were very adept with the pure as well as the mutant forms of the Spanish Colonial Revival.

Into this eclectic anthology modern architecture made its entrance during the late Twenties and early Thirties. Unfortunately, its arrival in southern California coincided with the onset of the Great Depression. If the economic retrenchment meant the end of palatial fantasies for movie

Mayan cinema

moguls, it also meant that for the average household the *Existenzminimum* henceforth became the affordable norm. With the patronage of the Lovells excepted, the Depression gave scant opportunity for modern architecture to show its full potential in southern California. Instead, it made the best of a shoe-string budget.

This meant that architects were now seriously competing with developers – acknowledged and past masters in the business of building quickly, efficiently, and cheaply. With the climate of southern California granting a building material's respectability even to waxed cardboard, modern architecture had little to teach the developers except the simplification of plan and form. Once this was learned by the builders, a connoisseur's eye for modern architecture was needed to detect and discriminate original works from the vulgarised bungaloids, ranchburgers, hillburgers, beachburgers and shackburgers fighting the bougainvillaeas for sun and air.

With the developers providing cheap and decent housing, the social mission of modern architecture was pre-empted in LA. With the climate undermining the need for craftsmanship and careful building techniques, the area for an architect's contribution to residential construction was limited even further. And since few architects have egos strong enough to seek commissions for self-effecting background buildings, many took solace in the romantic pose of the architect as a fearless innovator of form. For this reason we find the wide spectrum of professional cleverness in southern California, which purveys everything from J Lautner's saccharine and ingratiating gestures to F Gehry's architecture of punk. Amateur designers and do-it-yourself architects are not to be forgotten since they further enliven the scene by foisting daydream and nightmare houses on LA.

Given LA's prevailing backdrop of impermanent frame and stucco housing, the formal extravaganzas noted above catch and hold attention as the only available visual anchors — not for their exceptional merit, but for the context's vapid banality. But when the visual anchors are examined in detail, all too frequently they dismay thoughtful observers as shabby constructions and as pretentious conceptions. No wonder that LA frustrates visitors with reminiscences of older, denser, more substantial cities still fresh in their minds.

Finally, in contrast to European cities old enough to have acquired and not yet squandered their endowment of urbane settings and memorable public spaces, Los Angeles lacks areas with an arresting sense of place. The predicament arises not only in the world-wide fixation on suburbia but also in modern architecture's tendency to neglect urban design and to disregard the need for finely-tuned physical planning. As these conditions are not unique to southern California, and the evidence for this contention abounds in the newer districts of European cities, Los Angeles serves as an expansive, full-scale example of the urban environment wrought by contemporary Western civilisation: the cities of our immediate future are fast becoming expressway networks isolating clusters of free-standing buildings — most mediocre, some eye-catching and titillating, but precious few worth taking seriously.

Mission San Luis Rey

Grauman's Chinese Theatre

Coca Cola building

Crossroads of the world

Shrine auditorium

J Paul Getty Museum

The Brown Derby

Pan Pacific auditorium

The darkroom

Stefanos Polyzoides
THE SOURCES

It is our assertion that a number of architects practicing in Southern California in the first 30 years of the 20th century can be rightfully considered the sources of a new emerging attitude towards Architecture. The essence of this re-orientation of Architecture beyond the revivalist sphere of influence was based on three basic assumptions: that an Architecture appropriate to Los Angeles had to be based on local living sensibilities and contextual opportunities; that the constructive possibilities of the age were a critical aspect of a modern architectural aesthetic; that the organisational and stylistic structure of buildings was to be sympathetic to regional formal traditions.

The five architects we chose to present as the sources of such a local modern architectural orientation are: the Greene Brothers, Irving Gill, Frank Lloyd Wright, R M Schindler and Richard Neutra. They were architects that were capable of defining extraordinary personal modes of expression, never establishing deep ties with each other. They were individuals who belonged to different generations, had wholly different social and educational backgrounds and were not patronised by the same clients. Despite their adherence to personal canons of modernity, they precipitated very diverse effects on the Southern California urban environment.

The Greenes practiced a domestic architecture in wood based on vernacular images, which was widely emulated by the common builder.

Irving Gill is best know for his minimalist aesthetic based on reinforced concrete technology, primary forms and the underemphasis on surface as an active architectural ingredient. His later work is often ambiguous in its connection to revivalist precedents, especially the Missions and other early Spanish colonial buildings in Southern California. What is less known is his earlier work (up to 1906), which focused on a variety of style but always remained concerned with local materials and compositional attitude appropriate to context.

Frank Lloyd Wright used his local commissions in order both to extend his formal tendencies and also to give this region his image of an appropriate architecture. Of the five sources, he is the least socially and culturally connected to Southern California. The influence of his work beyond his son Lloyd and R M Schindler was minimal. And his sense of style fit for a modern Los Angeles was not strictly revivalist but unabashedly sentimental. The pursuit of the pre-Columbian roots of southwestern form came just short of the excessive surface manipulations of the eclectics.

R M Schindler was a rare mixture of a European student of the Wagnerschule, schooled in the atelier of Frank Lloyd Wright, the sole American master of his time.

Gill 'Cube House'

Schindler, Lovell Beach House

Neutra, Lovell House

Greene and Greene, Gamble House

Frank Lloyd Wright, Ennis House

Gill's architecture and his career as an architect are strongly conditioned by the social environment that he operated in. A man of limited education and narrow architectural training, he was nonetheless a person with deep intellectual and emotional capacities. He arrived in San Diego in 1893 after two years of apprenticeship with Sullivan in Chicago and was involved in a number of partnerships that practiced in a mildly eclectic style. His work was always concerned with local conditions and qualities and his professional success as an architect speaks for his popularity within the confines of a small frontier town. His work fit the aesthetic expectations of the San Diego elite but was hardly distinguished.

Throughout his early work there is evidence of continuous simplification and refinement of both space and detail. The process of clarifying and crystallising an aesthetic out of a series of confused and undistinguished buildings must have been very trying indeed. In a brief partnership with Frank Mead after 1906 he develops forcefully the idea of buildings composed of strong primary cubic forms that capture the light in their white surfaces and act as backgrounds to landscape and foregrounds to the sky. It is this process of focusing on a convincing overall formal framework that finally allows him to break through and develop a series of buildings that are extraordinary as sources to this region and stand on their own as powerful examples of American architecture. The serenity and power of Gill's forms are akin to those of Loos in Europe, but the aesthetic is diametrically opposed. Loos' work is sophisticated, urban, contradictory and almost self-deprecating. Gill's is rustic, rural, direct and obvious, optimistic and naive in a way that only a Western American architect could be at the turn of the century.

Gill's work is not supported by a verbal rationale. It is old-fashioned architecture combining design and construction and excluding previous theoretical intention or post-rationalisation. In this sense his work is archetypically Southern Californian. He proceeded to develop his work in a direction that has rarely been emulated in the west, thrusting his aesthetic upon issues of low-cost housing and public institutions of major importance. His vision was austere, virtuous and appropriately formed within the resources of a modest frontier.

The Dodge House was perhaps his most important single house. In it he managed to blend his concern for purity and a singular reading of form with his practical experiments in concrete construction and with his vital concern with landscape as an extension of building. The recent destruction of the house robbed American culture of a major monument; the Dodge House was a place to return to in order to understand the finest crevices of the turn-of-the-century American mind. Even the house's memory is capable of animating the imagination.

The public rooms of the Dodge House were severe in their finishes with most detail eliminated and with surface colour — most often elaborations on white — being the only means of changing the quality and mood of rooms. The incorporation of arches was seen not only as a necessary structural formal expression of the building but also as a way of enhancing its publicness and ennobling its mundane urban meaning. The massing of the building breaks down the overemphasis on formality, frontality and monumentality and brings the idea of house back into the building. The rooms inside the Dodge House are strung along informally with no articulated relationship pursued. The sections are simple and undifferentiated. The architectural expression is markedly anticlassical, almost iconoclastic, because the author utilised classical proportions and occasional classical organisational principles, as with the relationship between living room and garden and the references to historical buildings of California such as the Missions.

In the final analysis, Gill's work is incomplete and unresolved, processal and experimental, but highly sensitive to place-making in a western American world in need of civilisation and refinement. His understanding of local climate, materials, flora and his respect for local ways of life allowed him to complete his work, by making it simple and accessible in terms of meaning and hospitable in terms of place-making. His contribution must be urgently re-evaluated.

Stefanos Polyzoides

DODGE HOUSE, 1916
IRVING GILL

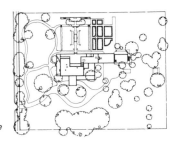

Site plan Dodge House

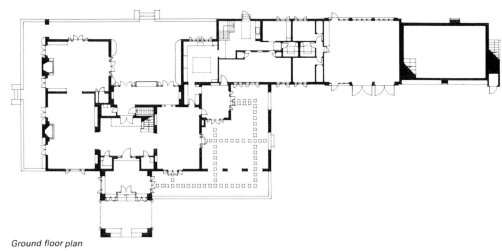

Ground floor plan

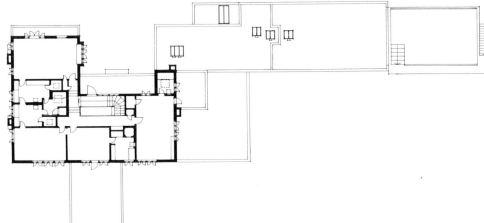

First floor plan

Entrance Hall interior

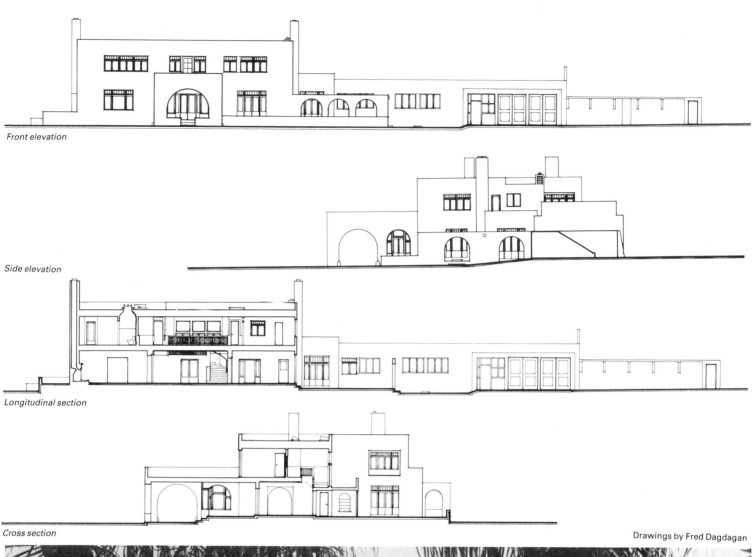

Front elevation

Side elevation

Longitudinal section

Cross section

Drawings by Fred Dagdagan

Garden view, Dodge House

Tiffany glass

Randell L Makinson
GREENE AND GREENE

In 1905 Charles Greene described the variety of California houses as 'a union of a Franciscan Mission with a Mississippi Steamboat'. The freedom and spontaneity of California life had prompted some bizarre experiments in style. At the same time, young architects like Charles and Henry Greene were inspired by the quiet valleys and rugged mountains, by the scorching sun and cooling sea breezes. All around them they found abundant building materials — fine woods from the north, cobblestones from the nearby arroyos, sand, stone and brick from local brickyards. Out of the contrast between the imported styles and ideas and the natural beauty of the environment, Architects Greene and Greene developed their own distinct design concepts, and their California Bungalow style changed the landscape of Southern California.

Greene and Greene reached back into the mid-19th century to the Bengalese houses of India. From these fundamentals they created a distinct, rich and creative American style. Their philosophy was simple and direct. They combined the 'climate, environment, materials available, and the habits and tastes' of their clients to produce some of the most appropriate domestic architecture in the country. Their early bungalows were small, modest houses which nevertheless exuded a dignity and charm usually associated with more expensive dwellings. The primary vocabulary was wood. Building and site were one. Natural materials were softened with subtle earth-toned stains. Structural elements hinting of the Japanese were boldly expressed and their identity emphasised by dramatic transitions when one element met another. Broad gabled roof lines and the rhythm of the articulated wood structure are reminiscent of the Swiss chalet. Yet as the Greenes moved away from the tight English plan to their more open courtyard plans, there were suggestions of the early California adobe *haciendas*.

While Greene and Greene are primarily identified with their shingle and wood-timbered structures, they expressed their convictions equally well in brick, gunite, wood and stucco — materials which were locally available and even more appropriate to Southern California than wood. Unfortunately these houses and their innovative plan compositions have been over-shadowed by the larger and more elaborate masterworks of the years 1907-11, for which they are most widely noted.

However, times were changing. The popularity of their earlier one- and two-storey bungalows had prompted many imitations by builders who did not understand the principles underlying the Greene designs and therefore produced very inferior copies. As a result, the demand for wooden bungalows declined. Nevertheless, the Greenes' emphasis on superb craftsmanship, the choice of only the finest materials, their creative imagination and attention to detail which extended to every aspect of house — furnishings, hardware, lighting and landscaping — have placed them among the leading exponents of the Arts and Crafts movement in America.

Gamble House 1908, side elevation, north

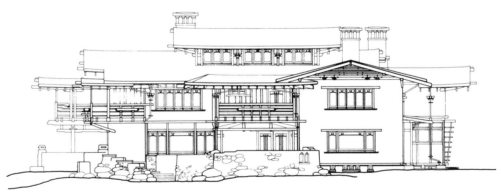

Rear elevation, west

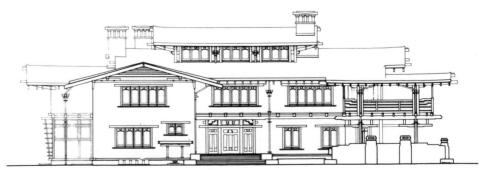

Front elevation, east

The David and Mary Gamble house of 1908, best preserved of Greene and Greene's major works, was named a National Historic Landmark by the United States Department of the Interior in 1978.

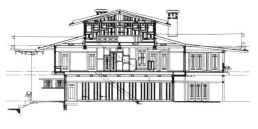

Section

Second floor plan

Ground floor plan

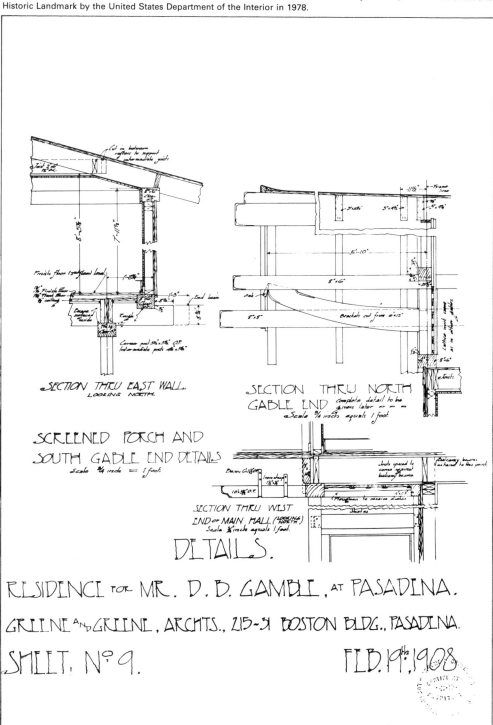

Gamble House, original details

Gamble House forward terrace and sleeping porch

Gamble House 1908

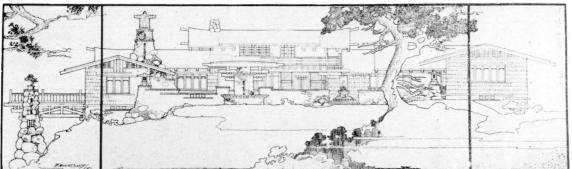

Illustration from Allen's 'Bungalow Booklet', 4th Edition, 1912

Detail of rear terrace

Entry hall

Gamble House 1908, front elevation

Exterior corner detail

Dining room

Metal strap details

Fern stand – living room

Entry porch panels (Emil Lange)

Interior stained glass window

THE LOVELL BEACH HOUSE, c 1926
R M SCHINDLER

The Lovell House is Schindler's best known building and the one that has been acknowledged by the critics as his most important. Without doubt the emphasis placed on this object reflects the European and Eastern American bias of valuing polemical and didactic buildings as the clearest representation of Modern Movement dogma.

The Lovell House is the last important building that Schindler produced, bearing the direct and literal influence of his schooling in Vienna and apprenticeship in Chicago. It is also his most complete effort at defining a doctrinaire architecture *de nuovo*. In the programmatic pronouncements of his celebrated client, the health physician Dr Phillip Lovell, in his own hypersensitive responses to contextual forces, his traditional reliance on light and structure as a definer of space, the complex multi-layering of exterior and interior spaces, in the emphasis on furniture and equipment as extensions of the building form, Schindler generated an idea that responded to the mid-20s efforts of the moderns to invent autonomous objects in order to nurture a modern (and superior) way of life. And his special contribution lies in the fact that the Lovell House is not only the carrier of conceptual intent but also a pleasant and fulfilling set of places capable of sustaining human life in the fullest sense of the word.

Schindler's subsequent work beyond 1926, and especially beyond the crash of 1929, changed significantly in direction and alienated many critics who had considered him a soldier and missionary for Modern Architecture in the wild west. His consequent ostracism from the history books followed as a natural result of his revisionist positions vis-à-vis the German-Dutch-French mainstream of the movement. The post-Lovell Schindler position was characterised by an increased sense of freedom from conceptual rigidity and the pursuit of perceptual, if not occasionally picturesque, ends. He accepted the economic dictates of the wood frame and stucco construction process and developed an aesthetic that took full advantage of its potential. Structure was suppressed at all costs and surface along with light became the dominant definers of space. His houses became more theatrical in their massing, and the plan disappeared as a generating force at the expense of the section and the elevations that it enclosed.

His method and process of work became increasingly intuitive, non-rational, and experimental. He designed buildings as fragments of ideas and used them as means to carry out his doubts and hopes. In opposition to the exclusivist aesthetic of the Modern Movement in the 1930s, Schindler's work was full of the vigour and energy that is generated by genuine attempts to engage the architectural unknown. The variety and inconclusiveness of his research prefigured the intellectual climate of architecture in the 1970s.

The Lovell House was generated by its owners as an image of what a 'healthy' life-sustaining object should be. The weekly column of Dr Lovell in the Los Angeles Times, on health of the body and mind, advocated regimes based on diet, exercise, habitat, and intellectual and emotional development that only became a reality in the California of the 1960s and 70s. Schindler authored six articles in Lovell's column in 1926, explaining the place of the house in a healthy life. The programmatic force of the Lovells on their house was paramount and highly suitable to Schindler.

The object itself was generated through the sectional transposition of five concrete frames. The frames are capable of defining hierarchical space within the confines of the building in response to a fictional context. (The house was built on sand dunes before the definition of an urbanised ground.) It prefigured the differences between the boardwalk and beach side where the two-storey living room is located, the street side where the arcade dominates, the alley side where the services are clustered, and the adjacent lot where the building is allowed to open to a garden/side yard. The frames are also capable of defining horizontal differentiation within the house. The ground is left in its natural condition. The public floor is removed from the street to the second floor and allowed a great beach view. The private floor is oriented to the

Interior with staircase

street and the last level, the roof garden, is afforded beautiful panoramic views of Newport Beach and the ocean.

The wood infill between frames generates an exquisite array of surfaces that separate, define, and mould space with no particular differentiation between their interior and exterior location. Treatment of detail is complex and insistently carries meaning down to tiny building parts. Surfaces instruct and communicate and are also capable of acting as mute backdrops. The furniture completes the house. Whether built-in or free-standing, it defines space

and reinforces its outward thrusts and inward articulations.

Schindler's effect on the Southern California scene diminished with his death in 1953. His work was intensely personal and his intuitive, private method was so removed from the dominant norms of a triumphant Modern Movement that it lacked local or international public. His value as a 'source' lies in his ability to illustrate amply the viability of a modern architecture as a means of improving life. The severe limitations of his architectural attitudes were really not his alone, but characterised his whole generation. *Stefanos Polyzoides*

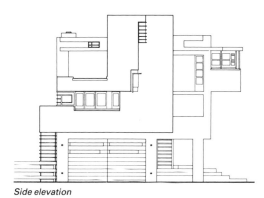

Side elevation

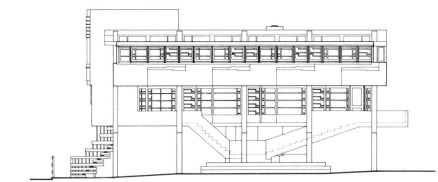

Front elevation

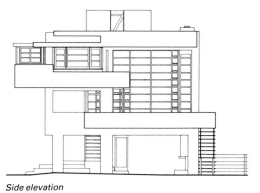

Side elevation

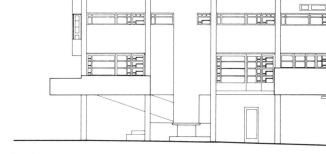

Rear elevation

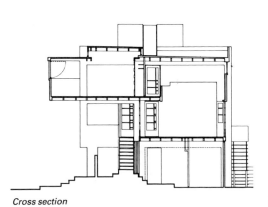

Cross section

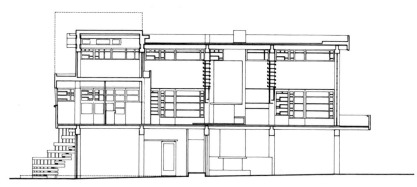

Longitudinal section

Lovell Beach House side elevation

View showing structural system

Close-up structural system

Design detail

Staircase detail

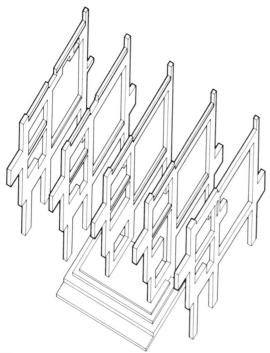

Diagram structural system

Corner detail

Close-up, structural detail

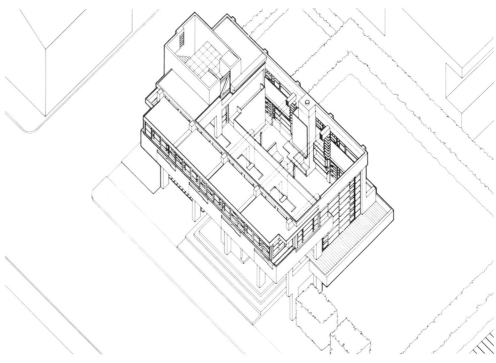

Cutaway axonometric showing first floor

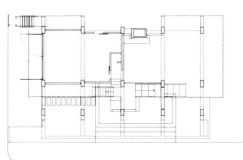

Ground floor

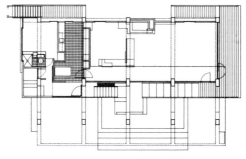

First floor

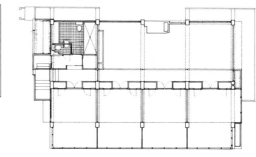

Second floor

Staircase detail

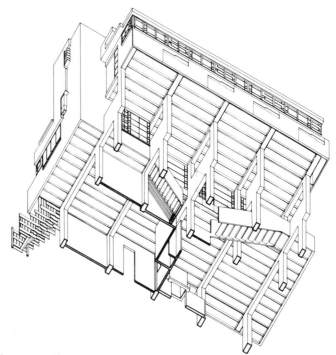

Axonometric showing structural form

Introduction

The concrete block houses of Los Angeles define a brief but important episode in Wright's career. They were conceived and executed during the years 1921 to 1924. Although later projects in the Twenties use a similar construction system, especially those for the Arizona Desert, the Los Angeles residences remain as the only executed work.

The Construction Method

The textile blocks, as Wright preferred to call them, have no precedent in his earlier work, although he experimented with conventional patterned blocks during the Teens in such efforts as Midway Gardens in Chicago. No doubt Wright felt the need to 'regionalise' his building materials and methods in Los Angeles. References to the architecture of Meso-America become apparent in delicate surface patterns, solidity of massing (including battered walls) and a preference for pyramidal compositions. All these qualities were uniquely suited to the concrete block system.

The blocks were precast on the site in special moulds, making it easy to achieve a great variety of surface patterns. In addition, glazing could be integrally cast within the block or these spaces simply could be left void. The blocks were assembled with steel rods, placed within the joints and subsequently grouted. The resulting mosaic thereby provided a cross-weave of reinforcing.

Planning

The Block Houses came at a time in Wright's career when his residential work suffered from a general stagnation. The Hollyhock House, while not employing the textile block, was the first evidence of the reinvigorated direction his work would take using the new construction method. Even though the Block Houses repudiate the plastic expression of the Prairie Houses, they are nonetheless indebted to them for certain planning principles.

An analysis of these residences reveals that fragments of the cruciform have been incorporated into all the projects. Most noticeable is the configuration of the living and/or dining rooms projecting at right angles to the main body of the house. The living zone is honorifically treated, being formally, if not symmetrically arranged with its large interior space externally expressed as a swelling volume with special block patterns and deep shadowed recesses. Secondary spaces such as services and bedrooms adhere rather informally to the sides or rear. However, the stabilising force of the composition is always the living area — a formula which can be traced back to such early works as the Martin House of 1904.

Siting

All the concrete block houses inhabit sites with pronounced slopes. This fact is interesting if one considers that vast areas of flat land were available for development and could logically have suited a Wrightian imperative to respond to the 'natural' landscape of the Los Angeles basin. Spectacular views certainly were a prime consideration for building on hillsides, however, another less obvious reason for this preference could have been Wright's bias for an architecture conceived in the round rather than frontally. Simply phrased, it may be that Wright's development of the diagonal in plan carried over quite logically to the diagonal in section.

There are two basic site types. The first of these is characterised by a tendency to stretch the building mass parallel to the contours of the slope. Terraces on both the uphill and downhill side provide a double prospect. The Storer and Ennis Houses define this type in its purest form. The second type redirects its energy by thrusting the building mass perpendicular to the contours. The living/dining rooms always occupy this honorific projection, following closely the example of the Hardy House of 1906. Both the Freeman House and La Miniatura fall into this category.

Two of the three Doheny Ranch Projects, shown above, can be viewed as hybrids, embracing in varying degrees characteristics of both aforementioned types. The third, House 'C', constitutes a further variation in that it spans a ravine, creating a dam-like wall. The central living room curves inward while the terrace opposite expands outward, resulting in a baroque interplay of convex and concave.

Ennis House corner detail

LA BLOCK HOUSES, 1921–1924
FRANK LLOYD WRIGHT

Conclusion

The ingenuity of Wright's block system conceals serious faults. First of all since the blocks were made individually on the site, construction became a time-consuming, demanding exercise. Consistent quality was difficult to achieve in the concrete and this has resulted in uneven weathering and crumbling of most external surfaces. Secondly, the reinforcing was often inadequately covered with mortar or became easily exposed with uneven earth settlement. Today some walls lack reinforcing altogether because of prolonged oxidation of the steel; they are held in place only by the binding strength of creeping vines which have entered the crevices.

The concrete blocks as a constructional experiment seem somewhat akin to Wright's infamous furniture — the effort is always more successful as a *plastic idea* than as a solution to *pragmatic fact*.

Jim Tice

Notes

1   Doheny Ranch Development, Sierra Madre Mountains, near Los Angeles (1921)

2   'La Miniatura', Millard House, Pasadena (1923)

3   Storer House, Los Angeles (1923)

4   Ennis House, Los Angeles (1924)

5   Freeman House, Los Angeles (1924)

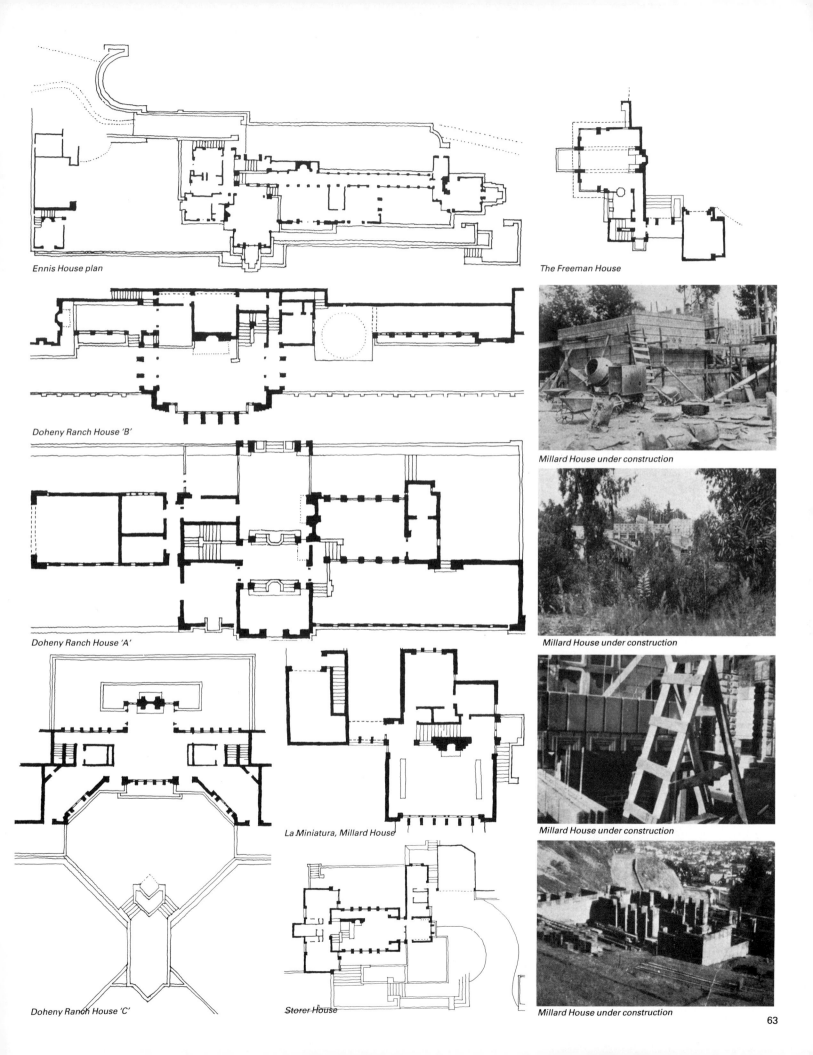

Ennis House plan

The Freeman House

Doheny Ranch House 'B'

Millard House under construction

Doheny Ranch House 'A'

Millard House under construction

Doheny Ranch House 'C'

La Miniatura, Millard House

Storer House

Millard House under construction

Millard House under construction

63

Ennis House, entrance area

Ennis House, detail of blockwork

Ennis House, view of LA from terrace

Ennis House

Ennis House, corner detail

Ennis House

Ennis House, block detail

Ennis House, long view

Ennis House, gate detail

65

THE LOVELL HEALTH HOUSE, 1929
RICHARD NEUTRA

Lovell House 1929

House under construction

Neutra's Lovell Health House was his first and most important building. By 1929, he had written extensively about the promise of the new architecture and about the constructive possibilities of the new age. He had completed his studies in Vienna and apprenticed with Mendelsohn in Berlin and Wright in Teliesin. He had collaborated with Schindler in Los Angeles for years. The Lovell House allowed him to translate his theoretical pronouncements into form and firmly established his reputation as a star of the new international Modern Movement.

Despite later changes in Neutra's attitudes and a steady development of his architectural sensibilities towards a reconciliation with the dictates of regional form, his most significant contributions are clearly German in inspiration and execution. Not only did he come to the US in order to build on the basis of continental perceptions of America as a paradigm of a progressive, future-oriented society, but he also kept that posture alive by continuous contact with Europe. His presence in the US tended to reinforce his perceived positions as a pioneer modern architect, capable of building according to a new dream, in a foreign land, buildings of a scale still unrealised in Europe.

The audacity of the Lovell House and its polemical quality in the developing German canons of modernism solicited immediate comment among Neutra's European colleagues and critics. The completed building was presented as the first house ever built in an industrial material (steel frame), incorporating a variety of mechanical and electrical gadgets widely admired abroad as symbols of progress. The scheme was skilfully handled to support the basic conceptual fixes of German modernism — dematerialisation of surface, articulation of structure, emphasis on fluidity and horizontality of the space, the tentative nature of an object's connection to the ground. Furthermore, certain modern biases in composition, such as compulsive asymmetry and irregularly modulated spatial sequences, were carried out to perfection. The Lovell House projects exhibited a unique combination of qualities: it was a sophisticated achievement and at the same time a naïve attempt at a new architecture, a much admired — if quite schizophrenic — modern condition.

So powerful an image was represented by the Health House that in its time it ranked with the Villa Savoye as the most convincing illustration of the viability of modernism both to accommodate and define the machine age. The building is generated by a columnar grid which is rarely visible and which defines three basic activity floors. The top one is reserved for bedrooms and private studies, the middle for the family's public life and the bottom for recreation. The most dominant and dramatic spatial feature of the building is the approach, entrance and descent into the living room. The living room itself is rather anti-climatic; it is overly horizontal in its proportions and hardly suggests place. The vertical surfaces of the building are not conceived of as continuous and interrelated. Therefore, interior elevations are discontinuous and flat. The exterior of the building is wrapped in a tight stucco and glass skin and is given an intensely horizontal expression, its thinness accentuated by steel windows and surface mounting of all openings. The degree of the control and consistency of intention of the exterior surfaces remarkable.

If the building is expressive of the arrogance and potential of a new and iconoclastic architecture, it is also a mirror of its shortcomings. The Lovell House was valued as an industrialised object, and yet the steel frame is nowhere visible and the material quality of the object vascillates between massive primitive wall and void as suggested by glass. The aesthetic expresses rational and orderly thinking, and yet the object is intuitively generated and quite arbitrarily fixed in its exact and particular design. The pursuit of house as healthy backdrop degenerates in points into continuous, unhierarchical and uncharged space. The new life is left dangling in a state of placeness where the only references are to architecture as an autonomous discipline and to the productive forces that sustain it (Model 'T' Ford headlights in the stairways).

The building attracted enormous attention here and abroad. It is extraordinarily elegant and photogenic, especially when viewed from the downhill side. It was made to incorporate all the ingredients of modern aspirations and both clients and students flocked to Neutra as a spokesman for the New Architecture. He built a lucrative practice on the Lovell House and he left an indelible mark on the professional map of the city in the 1930s, 1940s and 1950s. His office became the workshop where most of the strong architects of the generations apprenticed. The modern aesthetic, with all its questionable claims to novelty of form and intensified experience, was forcefully practiced from the Glendale Blvd office until Neutra's death in 1968.

The architectural ideology of Neutra was western in that it closely followed economic and material processes in their local development and treated architecture as an expression of those processes. Neutra's later work dealt conclusively with Western ways of life and sensibilities, but never came to terms with the issue of regional formal precedent. Currently, as the forces of reaction to the Modern Movement gain ground in their pursuit of form with historical connections, Neutra has lost his standing as a source relevant to the present. Nevertheless, he remains a figure whose contributions merit acknowledgement and admiration for the mastery of an Architecture, however limited in scope.

Stefanos Polyzoides

Corner detail 1929

Interior living area

General view

Corner detail with pool

Balcony area

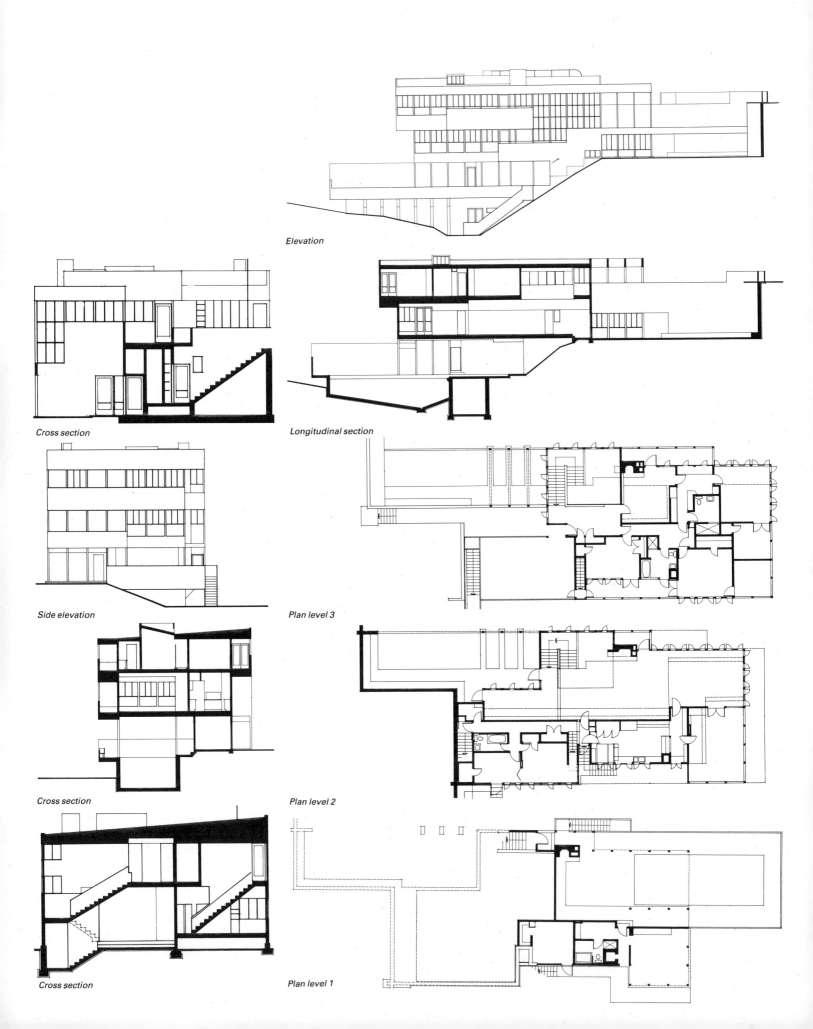

Elevation

Cross section

Longitudinal section

Side elevation

Plan level 3

Cross section

Plan level 2

Cross section

Plan level 1

Internal corner

View of the interior

General view

Staircase

Detail entrance area

Richard Berry
VILLAGE GREEN

Experience in a 38 year-old planned neighbourhood can yield lessons applicable to 'new community' planning of today.

With the advent of federal programmes, the debate on planned communities required refocusing on those specific problem aspects that are inherent in such a development approach. Large-scale applications of the concept – such as Reston, Virginia; Columbia, Maryland; Irvine, California; and others are formal symbols of planned communities but their purported attributes of viability and innovation will have to face the test of time before truly reliable evaluations can be made. There are, however, a number of early experiments that are potential laboratories from which lessons applicable to present-day problems of planning and development might be learned.

One example of a planned neighbourhood (as distinct from 'new town' or 'planned community') is Baldwin Hills Village, now nearly 40 years old. Located in the midst of vast tracts of single- and multi-family units that have grown up around it in southwestern Los Angeles, Baldwin Hills Village, consisting of 627 rental units, has had a 100 per cent occupancy record from the beginning and a constant rental waiting list. Also, in marked contrast to more recent encroaching projects, it has withstood physical deterioration, maintained an environmental identity; and through its subtle but sensible design for livability, has continued to attract middle- and upper-middle-income residents for whom it was intended in the 1940s with the difference that fewer of the present tenants are families with young children. (This difference could indicate either that original families have stayed to 'age' along with the Village or that, over the years, a change in kind of new families moving in has occurred.) Furthermore, though the amount of land devoted to community park – the 'Village Green' – appears extravagant to some, the project represents today a reasonable investment: having passed through a change of ownership, it was subsequently repurchased by the original developer.

Paradoxically, despite its successes (which include superb solutions for accommodating 20th-century automobile demands and Southern California's climate-generated way of living) the Village has not been reproduced nor emulated elsewhere, except in superficial aspects. Nor did it effectively influence the level of development of the urban environment around it.

The result of more than three years of intensive collaborative efforts, Baldwin Hills Village crystallised many of the planning experiments undertaken in the 1920s. The seminal concept stemmed from Radburn, New Jersey, the first planned community in America that utilises super-block to effect a separation of automobile from pedestrian and contains integral shopping and school facilities. (Comprehensive details and design philosophy are provided by Clarence Stein, the planner for both Radburn and Baldwin Hills Village, in his book, *New Towns for America*, Reinhold, 1957). The 80-acre site for the Village had been located in the mid-1930s and deemed feasible for a rental-unit neighbourhood. But detailed studies, not begun until 1938, faced innumerable delays due to

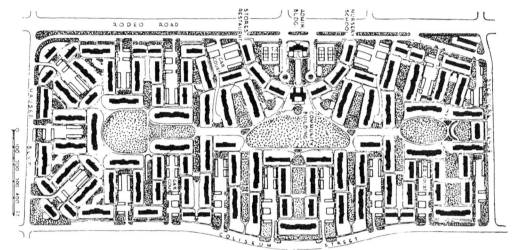

Site plan for Baldwin Hills Village – a residential super block of 627 units. Net area of land – 68 acres

conflicts with local and federal agencies. The final solutions ultimately necessitated one nonsensical street separating the commercial facilities from the residential. This north-south street along the eastern edge of the Village clearly demarks the end of one zoning classification and the beginning of another – which may have been the reason the city insisted on it – but it also destroys continuity and harmony between the Village and the commercial area as far as landscaping, pedestrian movement, and the handling of traffic and parking are concerned. This left about 1100 × 2500 feet (68 net acres) free of automobile traffic, with the rental units oriented inward to the Village Green. The original intent was also to incorporate an elementary school site by expanding the development, in a second stage, to a size capable of supporting the facility, but this proved unfeasible and the school eventually was located, unfortunately, on the opposite site of a busy arterial street across from the Village.

Parking adequacy and access needs were always central to the programme. As a result, the Village is one of the few examples of multi-family housing anywhere with a realistic parking ratio: three spaces per living unit. Each household has available one garage space; open space; and one guest space at curb indentations. (Though Federal Housing Administration and zoning regulations may pretend to ignore guest-parking problems, tenants 'voting' their preference in the open housing market do not; waiting lists are good ballot indicators!) All vehicles access is relegated to the periphery of the super-block by the skilful placement of private service driveways, which separate the cars and delivery trucks from pedestrian circulation paths. By providing a service road on the north side, the designers achieved their objectives of controlling circulation and of buffering the units from the nuisances generated by heavy traffic. In fact, by accepting and providing for automobile realities and without ignoring

either tenant convenience or potential dangers, the key objectives of relating all units to an interior park was rendered more reasonably achievable.

Another major premise was to create a quiet park within which the residents could have the sense of privacy and openness associated with single-family suburban estates. This dictated low-building ground coverage – 15 per cent – and an intimate building scale of one and two storeys. As a result the density approximates only ten units per net acre. But detached, individually-owned housing on their own lots in the suburbs surrounding the Village averages seven units per acre. With cluster or row housing, single family densities that match the Village could be achieved by investors in rental subdivisions. But such low density for rental units – from a point of development economics – undoubtedly is one factor that has prevented other entrepreneurs from using the Village as a prototype.

A cursory look at the neighbourhood and its residents as they have changed with time suggests still further lessons. The spatial relationships and vistas cannot be fully appreciated from word descriptions, plans, or even photographs. However, the serenity of the buildings and mature trees demonstrates how much the physical setting has been enhanced by nearly 40 years of aging. It has taken much of that time for the landscaping surrounding the 20-acre Green to achieve a true park character. The buildings, due to their simplicity, have a visual repose and undated quality that a more style-conscious architecture would have precluded. This suggests one of the most unequivocal criteria for new community budgeting that the Village example can illustrate. Its designers, by allocating only an approximate five per cent of the total construction cost to landscaping, could not be arbitrarily stylish with the living-unit exteriors; the result was the establishment of essential long-run neighbourhood assets. Landscaping and site planning accrue value with age; style sooner or later obsolesces toward a liability.

General view, Village Green

Pedestrian access routes

Wayfarers Chapel, Palos Verdes, California 1949, Lloyd Wright

Alson Clark
THE FORGOTTEN RATIONAL TRADITION

LA used to attract settlers. Now, when travel is so easy, it attracts visitors. Visiting architects love LA because it is a vast urban wasteland punctuated by exotic architectural follies ranging from the 'Craftsman' mansions of Greene and Greene to the pseudo-Andalusian cowbarns of the Mediterranean revivalists to the pseudo-Mayan revival fantasies of Wright and Stacey-Judd, and, to top it all off, such follies as the monumental Folk Art of the Watts Towers, the proto-pop wonders of Hot Dog stands shaped like Hot Dogs, a gigantic Super Graphic sign adorning the Hollywood Hills, and, as if this were not enough, a profusion of bland stucco apartments immortalised in the genre paintings of David Hockney. Visitors stimulated by this heady cultural *pot-pourri* are about as likely to look for sobriety as tourists in Las Vegas are prone to visit the YMCA.

But of course Southern California is not really an island, it is firmly attached to the western end of the United States. In the days before all the orange groves were filled with tracts and before the air was unhealthful for sensitive persons, people optimistically thought of LA as the first city planned to the scale of the automobile. Esther McCoy has summed up the way we used to look at our architectural-cultural relationship to the rest of the US by saying, 'But the modern movement was doing well: it had always done well in California from the time we more or less inherited it from Chicago at the turn of the century.'

Of course there was Gill, and after all, Wright had come here and, in the decade of the Twenties had built more buildings here than anywhere else. Not only that, his son Lloyd and his assistant Schindler had stayed and become resident architects, and Richard Neutra arrived as soon as he could.

Lloyd Wright (or more properly FLLW, Jr), the first modern to settle, had been in California for a decade when he built the Oasis, a hotel with shops in Palm Springs (1922). The style was industralised North African Mediterranean vernacular, the traditional mud being mixed with enough cement so that a monolithic structure was erected using technologically advanced 'slip-forms'. The influence of the Oasis was zilch, although Neutra *did* publish photographs in both his early German books on American architecture. The subsequent 'development' of 'Greater Palm Springs' was the LA region's greatest environmental disaster. In contrast, the Yucca-Vine market of 1928 had progeny. The first piece of LA architecture to use corrugated industrial siding as wall material started a tradition which flourishes today in the work of Frank Gehry, Helmut Schulitz and Peter de Bretteville.

In Lloyd's residential work his father annoyingly gets in the way. Lloyd struggled to find a mode of expression which would reconcile his own respect for the environment and love of plants with the family tradition of crisp,

disciplined geometry. When ornament was equated with crime, his use of patterned blocks as decorative elements seemed retrospective. Today it seems interesting.

The Swedenborgians who went to Lloyd after the war wanted an environment for worship with minimum protection from the elements. Before the landscaping grew the glass screen held in place by a minimum geometric frame, which seemed a sensitive machine-age restatement of the classic temple. The Wayfarer's Chapel' at last brought popular and professional recognition to LA's pioneer modernist.

In the early 1930s antipathy to modern was still so strong that those who chose to work in the Neutra office did so because they were already committed but needed training. Since schools were still Beaux-Arts this office was one of the only places to receive such training. Three of the young apprentices were Harwell Hamilton Harris, Gregory Ain and Raphael Soriano. Harris, a college sculpture major, had poured through the Wasmuth Monograph at the LA Public Library after discovering the LA work of Lloyd Wright and then his father. Ain had dropped out of USC in disgust and Soriano struggled through the school after epic battles with the faculty.

In 1934, when Harris built his first house, finding a cheap site was no problem; from Palos Verdes (which had been planned by Frederick Law Olmstead, Jr where he lived in retirement by the sea) to Pasadena, the hills had been laced with narrow streets which followed the contours of the hills. Due to the Depression, which halted building activity, the majority of the lots were empty. The first Harris commission, for Pauline Lowe, was built on a slight downslope in Altadena. The living-dining room was at the rear, to take advantage of the view and to relate to the major outdoor space. Each bedroom opened on to its own patio. The exterior was covered with barn-grade vertical redwood boards in the California vernacular tradition (revived later by Charles Moore at Sea Ranch) and the fences which made the bedroom patios private were of the same material. The front door opened off still another patio, access to which was through a passage between house and garage. The plan was modular, space flowed, outdoors and indoors were related and everything was consistently detailed. What had been created was a sort of little private world, only minimally related to the street and neighbourhood (the neighbours were probably not very interesting and you got out of the car if you wanted to see friends). Things of this sort had probably never before been available to people with ordinary incomes. It was a success. Those who didn't like the 'coldness' of modern loved the 'warmth' of Harwell Harris. Critics tried to decide how high an Art Form a cheap house could be. Harris answered them, and at the same time acknowledged that he wasn't making very much money by building himself a

classic one-room wood pavilion with practically no furniture in which he continued to live until he left California. He was tolerant of client tastes. His John Entenza house in Santa Monica Canyon (1937) is finished with white plaster, and has the inevitable International Style spiral staircase ascending to the roof.

Peter Blake has recently recalled that the New York Museum of Modern Art tried unsuccessfully to sell the public the International Style by peddling it as some kind of Patent Medicine, beneficial to your health. When this campaign failed MOMA began to note more carefully what was going on in the provinces, and decided that Harwell Harris was doing good work. His own house and the plan of the Pauline Lowe house were included in the book *Built in USA – 1932-1944*. For years after, L A got its fair share of attention in the architectural press.

The schools changed their attitude. USC became a training ground for architects who wanted to do the regional thing. Garrett Eckbo and others reworked the whole idea of landscaping so that people who couldn't afford gardeners could have pleasant environments. Whitney Smith and Wayne Williams became well-known for recreation buildings in the vernacular, and Gordon Drake refined the wood house in somewhat the same way that Pierre Koenig and Craig Ellwood refined the steel house. Calvin Straub, Conrad Buff and Don Hensman, in charge of design at SC, seemed to end the whole era in the late 1950s by being influenced by Greene and Greene, Frank Lloyd Wright and Richard Neutra all at the same time. Developers filled the region with coarsened versions of Harwell Harris, just as the outskirts of London were filled with insensitive adaptations of 'The Orchard', Chorley Wood, in an earlier era.

The best privately financed multiple-family housing of the 1930s and 1940s was the work of the second Neutra apprentice,Gregory Ain. The Dunsmuir Flats (they were not flats) consisted of four two-storey units with common walls, staggered and stepped up the slope, making each unit, which opened to a garden, as private as possible. MOMA discovered Gregory Ain at the same time it discovered Harwell Harris, and the Dunsmuir Flats were included in *Built in USA*. Recognition led to two interesting commissions after the war, ten staggered row houses and a tract of 100 houses in Mar Vista. All of them used the same plan, which made low-cost wood houses instantly flexible. By pushing movable partitions the houses could have three bedrooms, two bedrooms and a larger living room, or become quite spacious one-bedroom units. In the tract, variety was achieved by turning houses this way and that and by attaching garages at different points. Every dollar was spent on pleasant living. MOMA was so impressed that it commissioned Ain to build a replica in its garden. It was the last MOMA Demonstration House and

Wayfarers Chapel, Lloyd Wright

The Chemosphere, 1960, John Lautner

the last Ain tract commmission. Common sense and reticent good taste were not what developers wanted. Harwell Harris had accepted the Deanship at Texas in the early 1950s, and Gregory Ain, after some years on the faculty at USC, became Dean of Architecture at Penn State.

The third Neutra apprentice, Raphael Soriano, was a European, born on the island of Rhodes. He came to Neutra to learn the new technology, which he soon put to use building the most severe L A houses of the 1930s. The high point of his career before the war was the Hallawell Seed Company nursery in San Francisco, a design he saw as completely determined by the prefabricated 'Lattice-Steel structural system. By the time building had resumed after the war, he had added corrugated industrial siding and corrugated plastic to his vocabulary. His philosophy became more radical (the war was a time when the Brave New World seemed about to happen). He tried his best to be anonymous. A steel-box apartment house of the late 1940s now seems thin because Soriano, in contrast to Mies, used the minimum required steel in his frame. He built the first steel Case Study House. Pierre Koenig, who worked for him, and Craig Ellwood carried on the L A steel tradition.

J R Davidson had a European architectural training. After he arrived in L A in 1925 he demonstrated his skill in handling modern materials in commercial work. In his houses he paid the same attention to the details. The product tended to be a little severe, but by a logical step-by-step development he evolved into a Californian. He was never dramatic. His work became more open, horizontal and tranquil, rather than more bland.

Thornton Abell graduated in architecture from USC in 1931. He built for himself in Santa Monica Canyon in 1937, where he chose a steep downward slope with view to the South. It determined the form of his house, which steps down the hill, using the roof of the first level as a deck opening off the second, terminating in a third-level deck enclosed by a wall of horizontal redwood boards, used nowhere else in the building. It sounds jumbled, but is actually serene and exciting at the same time. Most of his subsequent work has this quality. The horizontal board wall was repeated in his office and in houses where the excitement comes from movement from a strongly lighted courtyard into a darker sheltering room. An Abell house (and houses by many other L A architects) could be described as 'laid back' and 'cool', but these have become contemptuous words to describe a part of the L A tradition which it seems better to sweep under the carpet because it doesn't jibe with the 'I found myself by moving to L A' myth. If you find that what you really want to do is take it easy, that's somehow upsetting.

John Lautner's career has been anything but serene. After six years with Frank Lloyd Wright he arrived in the late 1930s and built his own obligatory sensitive hillside house. He then did commercial work, in which he showed even more talent than Richard Neutra for going through Sweet's Catalog and picking out industrial materials to use as finishes, roofing, sunscreens and the like. As soon as he struck out on his own it became apparent that there were two John Lautners. He received a commission for a Drive-

In restaurant and an auto salesroom and repair shop which happened to be next to each other. The restaurant and repair shop, using corrugated aluminium and embellished here and there with things out of Sweet's, were superb, but the main showroom, which featured a gigantic steel frame almost touching the ground at one corner, was never completed, which was perhaps just as well.

Then came the Chemosphere House, with its beautiful top profile (the bottom beauty had to be dispensed with due to budget problems), a convincing demonstration of what could be done with unbuildable lots. At the same time, however, there was Silvertop, a mansion which the architect planned as if he were building a minimum house. The living and dining areas were combined (to get a feeling of greater space?). The principal way of getting from the dining area to the kitchen was to press a button which raised a solid brick wall up in the air. The large master bedroom could become even larger by pressing another button which moved the wall back a couple of feet. The bizarre half of Lautner's work seems 'relevant' to visitors to the Big Orange.

The generation of the 1930s, 1940s and 1950s left little mark on the fabric of the part of L A that was not the valleys. During the Depression they considered themselves lucky to get their modest commissions. The 1940s were chaotic, and, by the 1950s, the tradition of Civic Art had been thrown out along with the pediments and cornices. Old-timers groaned when another tract, no matter how hygenic, cancelled out another open space. Building shelter for a lot of people was socially useful, but you had to contend with laws written up by committees composed of fire inspectors who wanted wide roads for convenient access and civic boosters who wanted their town to have 'estate-size' lots. The 1930s client who had perhaps read Bruno Taut and saw his modern house as some kind of step towards a better world was pretty much out of the picture.

The achievement of the regional school (it was not regional in the Bay Area sense, and it wasn't really a school) was to create domestic buildings which would take full advantage of the new technology, the climate and the site, providing pleasant environments for ordinary people.

Bibliography

Esther McCoy *Case Study Houses 1945-1962* Second Edition, Hennessey & Ingalls, Los Angeles (1977), p1
Richard J Neutra *Wie Baut Amerika*, Julius Hoffmann, Stuttgart (1927), pp75,76
Amerika. die Stilbildung des neuen Bauens in den Vereinigten Staten, Verlag Anton Schroll, Vienna (1930), p119.
Peter Blake 'Architecture is an Art and MOMA is its Prophet'. *Art News*, NY, vol 78 no. 8, (October 1979) pp97-101
Elizabeth Mock, ed *Built in USA – 1932-1944,* The Museum of Modern Art, New York (1944), pp34-35
Ibid, pp52-53
The Museum of Modern Art – Woman's Home Companion Exhibition House. Gregory Ain architect, Joseph Johnson and Alfred Day collaborating. The Museum of Modern Art, New York (1950)

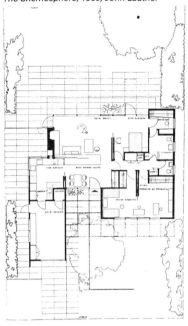

Museum of Modern Art, Woman's Home Companion Exhibition House, 1950, Gregory Ain with Joseph Johnson and Alfred Day collaborating.

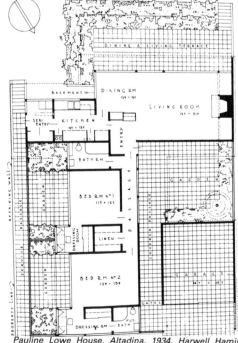

Pauline Lowe House, Altadina, 1934, Harwell Hamilton Harris and Carl Anderson

House by Thornton Abell

Sears Roebuck Garden Shop, 1947, Stiles Clements

Oasis Hotel, Palm Springs 1922–23, Lloyd Wright

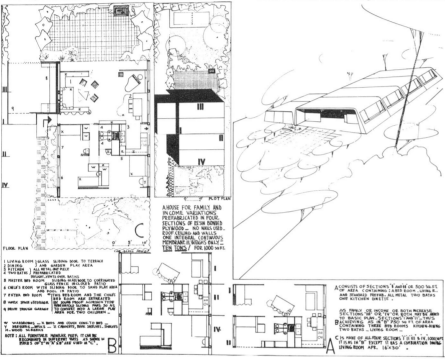

'Designs for Post War Living', Raphael Soriano, 3rd Prize

Ciro, Beverly Hills, Raphael Soriano and Serge Chermayeff

Drake House, 1946, Gordon Drake

Fellowship Park House, 1936, Harwell Hamilton Harris

Dunsmuir Flats, Los Angeles, 1938, Gregory Ain

EAMES HOUSE, PACIFIC PALISADES, 1949
CHARLES AND RAY EAMES

The Eames office has been a mystical oasis for most serious designers around the world for thirty years. Although their work in architecture has been minimal, their influence on architects has been extraordinary. Appropriately this unique couple were awarded the Royal Gold Medal of the Royal Institute of British Architects in 1979.

Many amazing things have happened in Los Angeles, but nothing for me as internationally stimulating has emerged from the celluloid city as the design legacy of the Eames office during the past all but forty years. The Eames talent defies classification. They are architects, inventors, designers, craftsmen, scientists, film-makers, educators. Yet in all their diversity, their creation is not a series of separate achievements but a unified aesthetic with the organic growth of a beautiful tree.

Much of the Eames imagery comes from the archives of American machinery or from standard catalogues of machined parts. These have been taken out of context and given an elegance; their appeal is the mixture of familiarity and surprise. There is a loyalty to family groups, a loyalty to their own special imagery. Today the number of refinements to existing pieces far exceeds the creation of new ones. But, as Konrad Wachsmann says 'the number of examples doesn't matter. In furniture the century is theirs.' Ten churches or one Brunelleschi has said it.

In 1949 the Case Study House became the component structure of the decade, still as breathtaking today as on the day it burst on the architectural world, still unsurpassed as a stage for living. The remarkable domestic scale of their design is lyrical in its setting on a beautiful site. Here the component chasteness of the frame and the richness of the interiors interact in much the same way as exhibitions and films react to structure and content.

Paul Schrader seems to isolate the essential Charles Eames when he describes him, in the broadest sense of the word, as a scientist. In the film introduction to the United States Science Exhibit at Seattle Fair, Eames defines that rare creature, the true scientist:

Science is essentially an 'artistic or philosophical enterprise carried on for its own sake'. In this it is more akin to play than to work, but it is quite a sophisticated play in which the scientist views nature as a system of interlocking puzzles. He assumes that the puzzles have a solution, that they will be fair, he holds to a faith in the underlying order of the universe. His motivation is his fascination with the puzzle itself, his method a curious interplay between idea and experiment. His pleasures are those of an artist. High on the list of prerequisites for being a scientist is a quality that defines the rich human being as much as it does a man of science – that is, his ability and desire to reach out with his mind and his imagination to seek outside himself.

Was this a conscious or an unconscious autobiography? In the case of the Eames, Da Vinci's Universal Man was happily superseded by the Eames' Universal Man and Woman. Forty years of instinctive harmonious work forged a partnership which has given supreme pleasure to the world.

Derek Walker

Two storey area

Interior

Table arrangement

Composition

Living area

View through

Skylight

Staircase detail

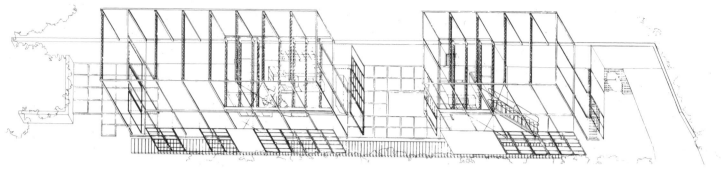

Axonometric (drawn by Charles Lee)

Pathway

Aspect

Landscape detail

External cladding

Corner detail

Oblique view

House through landscape

Cladding detail

House through landscape

Reflections

View from the house

Oblique view

77

LA HOUSES
A QUINCY JONES, 1913–1979

With the death of Quincy Jones in August, 1979, Los Angeles lost an architect of quiet integrity, whose contribution in the field of post-war housing was exceptional. The University of Southern California also lost a considerable spokesman, who had served as Dean of the School of Architecture and Fine Arts until persistent ill health forced his resignation. Esther McCoy's comments about aspects of his work seem appropriate in a section devoted to his work in housing:

I had always thought of Quincy as more of an environmentalist and humanist than a structuralist. This was because I respected so much his use of land in the post-war Mutual Housing, and later in his tract housing for Eichler Homes. He was one of the few to bridge successfully that chasm between the custom-built and merchant-built house, and in doing so performed a great service to the community and to architecture.

It is true that Eichler was an enlightened developer, but I saw Quincy's quiet persuasiveness and his patience in the design of the houses and the site planning – especially in the greenbelt plan which cut the size of lots and threw the surplus into small common parks. In and out of the classroom Quincy was an educator, and the quality of life was always a deep concern.

The Barn, interior

The Barn – converted in 1965 by Quincy Jones

Jones' Steel House, 1953

Jones' Steel House, patio view

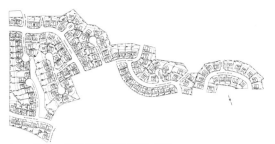

Layout Lucas Valley Eichler homes, 1961

Sketch by Quincy Jones, plan 2.4

Sketch by Quincy Jones, plan 1.4

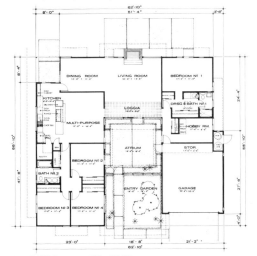

PLAN 2.4

4 BEDROOMS 2 BATHS 2135 SQ FT
GARAGE 500 SQ FT
ATRIUM 335 SQ FT
ENTRY GARDEN 333 SQ FT

GRAPHIC SCALE IN FEET

Plan 2.4 'Primewood' for Eichler

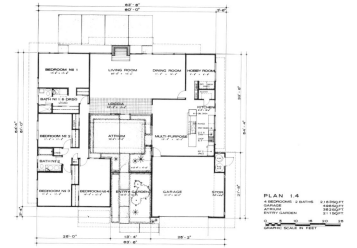

PLAN 1.4

4 BEDROOMS 2 BATHS 2183 SQ FT
GARAGE 495 SQ FT
ATRIUM 382 SQ FT
ENTRY GARDEN 211 SQ FT

GRAPHIC SCALE IN FEET

Plan 1.4 'Primewood' for Eichler

Atrium House for Eichler

Eichler Home

Eichler Home

Early Eichler Home

79

Stefanos Polyzoides, Roger Sherwood and James Tice

THE FABULOUS COURTYARD DWELLINGS OF ARTHUR AND NINA ZWEBELL

The real value of the courtyard housing of Los Angeles lies beyond its obvious and seductive qualities. Our research focuses equally on the recording of its physical character through measured drawings and detailed photographs as well as in the revelation of underlying principles which have been clouded by the doctrines of modern times. The lessons of the courts have not led us in the direction of a pursuit of shallow, stylistic nostalgia by association, or to a retreat from some of the unpleasant realities of modern life. Instead, they helped clarify the shortcomings of stereotyped notions about architecture and the architecture of housing. Strategies about how to achieve a collective of dwellings in a dense urban situation without destroying personal amenities of individual dwelling and garden, concepts about communal living, ideas about the relationship between the individual dwellings, the collectivity of dwellings, and the city itself all have potential for universal application.

The Zwebell Courts. Arthur and Nina Zwebell gave Los Angeles a unique building heritage in a burst of activity that lasted less than a decade. During the 1920s, this team designed and built several single family houses, but their fame will, without doubt, rest on eight or so buildings of a character peculiar to Los Angeles that we have termed 'courtyard housing'.

Arthur and Nina Wilcox Zwebell grew up in the Midwest. She was an avid musician and graduated from Northwestern University in 1914. He was a self-educated man – his formal education did not go beyond the eighth grade. Zwebell's talents for invention and design became apparent early in life through his first great passion, automobiles. Not only did he invent a version of the tire vulcaniser, but designed and produced a sporty roadster body to be attached to a standard Ford chassis. Three years after their marriage in 1914 the Zwebells travelled to Los Angeles while on vacation and returned in 1921 to live there permanently. They brought with them $35000 and the desire to build.

Arthur Zwebell immediately found himself a contractor. With the assistance of Nina, who did all the interiors, he designed and developed his first court, a Norman-style building, now destroyed, called Quaint Village. Arthur learned quickly. He proceeded to design and build a number of single-family houses. In 1922-23, his second court appeared in Hollywood in an astonishing 'Hansel and Gretel' fantasy style. Meanwhile, Nina established an interiors firm as well as a furniture factory, where she concurrently designed and produced period furniture throughout the 1920s. The Zwebells never operated an office as such but preferred to work out of their own house. Most architectural and design drawings were executed by them with occasional outside help. Architects and engineers were hired merely to sign necessary drawings.

The Zwebells' first known exceptional courtyard housing experiment was the Villa Primavera (also referred to as the Mexican Village). It was situated in a part of Hollywood where, in 1923, only one other house existed. The change in style to Spanish Revival in this work and in subsequent projects executed in the 1920s seems to be more a response to popular demand than to a doctrinaire architectural attachment to Mediterranean forms. For the

Interior Warner Apartment

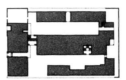

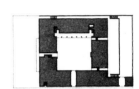

Plan typologies

first time we can see the essential ingredients of the developer courtyard housing type. The Spanish style wood-and-stucco structure completely surrounds a courtyard which is animated by a tiled fountain, outside fireplace and lush foliage. Parking is cleverly integrated into the overall design, in this case by incorporation into one side of the building mass. All ten housing units have their primary access and existence dependent upon the court. Interior zoning capitalises on views of the central space. Services are typically placed on exterior walls and away from the courtyard itself. The Villa Primavera is located on a corner site with major entrance set back and a minor entrance flush to the street. Its rambling appearance betrays a plan configuration that is nearly a perfect square. All but the two-storey east wing is on one level. The living units on this side are miniature in scale but still possess a certain charm — each has a corner fireplace, small niches, exposed timber ceiling, and tile floors. The dwellings on the opposing sides are somewhat larger and much more spatially complex — harbingers of the Zwebells' later development. After the completion of Villa Primavera, where the Zwebells themselves resided, a number of commissions quickly followed, including several houses in Pasadena and one for Harold Lloyd's mother next to the actor's estate in Beverly Hills.

In 1926, the Zwebells sold the Villa Primavera in order to develop their next court, the Andalusia. This extraordinary building firmly established their reputation. By now, Zwebell had mastered a daring and pure Andalusian style which was supported by an abundant array of craftsmen. The Andalusia is perhaps Zwebell's most accomplished building, as it incorporates the best features of all the experiments. Its overall form and the dwelling pieces are beautifully resolved. In Andalusia, the problem of parking on grade has been ingeniously resolved. The garages, if they may be called that, are two flanking pavilions on each side of a forecourt. The impression that one gets is one of three separate but exquisitely related outdoor rooms: one reserved primarily for the automobile which is off the street and paved; the second within the body of the court rendered as an Andalusian patio and directly related to the nine dwellings; and the third located in the most private part of the site, also finished in hard materials and reserved for recreational activities. The small archways cut into the body of the building heighten the sensation of spatial connection. The units continue the spatial experiments of the Patio del Moro, culminating in the Zwebell's own dwellings. Within is an extraordinary two-storey living space which was specifically designed to accommodate a pipe organ for Nina Zwebell. The Andalusia was (and continues to be) a favourite watering hole for aspiring and established members of the motion picture set. Some of its more famous residents: Cesar Romero, Clara Bow, John Payne, and Marlon Brando.

In 1927, the Zwebells acquired the land where they were to build their next major works, christened The Ronda. The Ronda's plan configuration is unique in the Zwebell *oeuvre*. The single, central court has been abandoned in favour of two linear spaces which, from certain vantage points, appear to be picturesque Andalusian streets. Certainly, the large size of the lot — about twice that

of the Andalusia — helped to determine this solution, which contains 20 units. Set directly against the street on the west is a continuous wall of dwellings which step from four storeys to two, with three lower apartment blocks running perpendicular. In between these building blocks, and at different levels, are some of the most wonderful exterior spaces to be found in Los Angeles. There are a great variety of dwelling units in The Ronda, including cottages, maisonettes with two-storey spaces and mezzanines, as well as some interesting split-level units. These latter were the result of the Zwebells' ingenious accommodation to the half-sunken basement garage to the north with the lower court to the south. Typically, Zwebell turned a knotty problem into an ingenious solution.

A year later, the Zwebells moved their building activity eastward, first designing the El Cabrillo in Hollywood, followed by the Casa Laguna in Los Felix. The El Cabrillo appears to be a judicious attempt to duplicate the Andalusia for a different site and in a different material. The massing of the two buildings is identical. But the El Cabrillo as a corner building was originally entered from both streets. Unfortunately, through continuous street-widening, the main entry has been closed altogether and building configuration on the sidewalk has been considerably altered. The El Cabrillo is not built in wood and stucco as is typical of virtually all the other Zwebell courts. Instead, a concrete block is used which is non-standard in size in an apparent attempt to create an adobe block effect. The ten units follow the Zwebell pattern of incorporating two-storey living rooms, mezzanines and graceful staircases. All the unit interiors are skilfully modelled in light with a variety of window openings. Especially effective are the small lunettes in the upper part of the living room space. The El Cabrillo was intended as a place for residence of both transient and permanent members of the Hollywood scene. One of the Talmage sisters lived here and Hollywood lore has the name of Cecil B DeMille's daughter connected with this building. And at least one of Rudolph Valentino's films is alleged to have used the El Cabrillo as a stage set.

Like the Primavera and the El Cabrillo, the Casa Laguna is located on a corner site. Its major entrance is set back considerably from the street, recalling a similar solution in the Primavera. Secondary pedestrian and vehicular access through separate entries occurs on the adjacent side. The automobile entry pierces through an extension of the main building to a lower paved court and row of garages located beneath a communal sun terrace. The square courtyard beyond contains the usual Zwebell features. What makes it special is its generous proportions for the 12 surrounding units. In addition, there is an elaborate two-storey loggia with intricate wooden capitals and store columns reminiscent of Andalusian prototypes such as the Casa del Chapiz in Granada. The underplayed exterior of the Casa Laguna belies unusual and complex interiors. The additional terrace on the west allows the units in this building a more varied and open exposure than in the 'earlier courts.

After the Courts. In 1929, with the complete collapse of the private housing market, the Zwebells turned to other occupations. They were first engaged as set designers in

the movie studios, later turning to furniture design and production. Arthur made an abortive attempt to return to building with a plan to manufacture a modular housing system in 1934-36. Unfortunately for Zwebell and the history of architecture, Los Angeles had to rely on sponsorship of the FHA during that economically troubled era. Even though his efforts proceeded to the point where he designed and built a prototype house, relations with the housing authorities were so difficult and bitter that after a storm damaged his housing plants in Van Nuys, he took his insurance in settlement and quit building. Except for three residences for his family in North Hollywood, he never practised architecture again. He died in 1973. Nina Zwebell died the next year.

The Zwebells' Contribution. Without doubt Arthur and Nina Zwebell were the original creators of the highly refined deluxe court in Los Angeles. However brief an interlude in the building history of this region, their contribution is extraordinary, with their concern for traditional urban form, their adaptation and development of the Los Angeles court-type of housing, the use of landscape as a discrete formal language, and the richness of the individual units in each court. Both Zwebells were consciously opposed to the forms of modern architecture and design. They were 'ancients' in the sense that they sought inspiration in the imagery of the past. This, however, is only a part of their story. For, paradoxically, Arthur demanded and finally achieved an architecture which in planning organisation was as rational as any truly modern work was supposed to be. We have only to consider the variety of ingenious parking solutions to dismiss once and for all any temptation to dismiss this work as that of a picturesque dilettante. This duality, then, can explain both Zwebells' devotion to the Spanish Mediterranean style and Arthur's audacious attempt at factory-produced housing. The Zwebells' control of projects from finance to construction and their unique combination of business and design skills generated a set of exemplary buildings that served as a standard for most examples of courtyard housing that followed. From our perspective today, their work is valid not only as a model for future housing experiments. It is also, in absolute terms, architecture of the highest quality — some of the finest ever built in Los Angeles.

Our forthcoming book, *Courtyard Housing in Los Angeles*, a typological analysis, contains the following materials:

- The importance of the courts to the culture of Los Angeles.
- Local and Mediterranean precedents for courtyard housing.
- An analytical framework for defining the complete typological range of observed court examples.
- Los Angeles courtyard housing as an example of a possible housing tradition, as a part of an attitude of making dwellings that contrasts sharply with received notions of 'Western housing' as practised in the last 100 years.
- A portfolio of 30 cases studies of deluxe courts, including drawings, photos and commentary. (The Zwebell excerpt published here constitutes a portion of this chapter.)

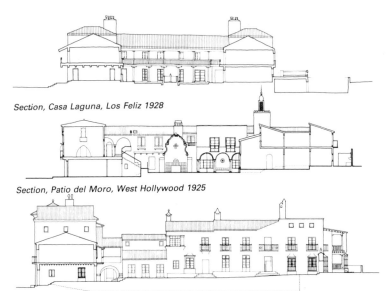

Section, Casa Laguna, Los Feliz 1928

Section, Patio del Moro, West Hollywood 1925

Elevation, The Ronda, West Hollywood 1927

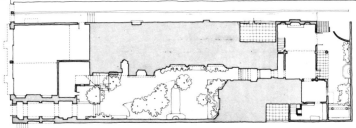

Plan, Patio del Moro

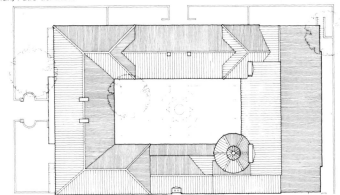

Roof plan, El Cabrillo, Hollywood 1928

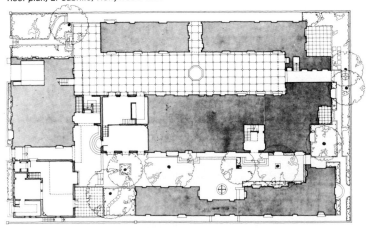

Site plan, The Ronda, West Hollywood

Internal court, The Ronda

Casa Laguna

El Cabrillo

Patio del Moro

Doorway, Patio del Moro

Arthur Zwebell

Nina Zwebell

Internal court, The Andalusia

Interior, Patio del Moro

Casa Laguna

Street entrance

Villa Primavera

Villa Primavera 1923

Patio del Moro

The Ronda

Interior, The Ronda

Interior, The Andalusia

Andalusia

Alson Clark

THE CASE STUDY PROGRAMME

The Modern Movement in Los Angeles was healthy in 1945. The small houses created by local talents before the war had shown that superior environments could be created for people of modest means. John Entenza realised that if his magazine, *Arts and Architecture*, could mount some kind of on-going programme to publicise the post-war houses that would be built, the advantages of the contemporary approach would become widely known. The magazine had no money of its own and there was no government subsidy. The houses were to be built and paid for by individuals. They would be subjected to the scrutiny of a critical public, so Entenza chose designers known for their attention to detail. The first modest, practical houses by J R Davidson and Thornton Abell had wood frames as steel was not available in the immediate post-war period.

The magazine *did* have the money to buy a site large enough for three Case Studies. Richard Neutra built one. Surprisingly he had actually come to like wood and this relaxed rambler was finished with board and bat. The second and third houses were planned and built simultaneously. The metal mullions, bracing and open-web joists of the Eames House give it the air of an American 'Maison de Verre' set down in virgin country. In the most unconventional single gesture of the program, the field in front of the house remained unlandscaped — this in an area where home landscaping is almost a religion. The Entenza house, by Eames and Eero Saarinen was a horizontal box which acted as a foil to the long, high, narrow Eames house across the field.

The programme got back on the social track with a three-bedroom steel pavilion by Raphael Soriano, who let the new technology speak for itself. The Ellwoods and Koenigs that followed have in retrospect become *the* Case Study houses. The Mies courthouse proved the ideal prototype for Ellwood to develop into lay-outs suitable for Los Angeles living. A new type of reinforced brick was played off against steel frames, which became thinner and more refined with each new development in technology. Some people like floating porches and others see them as flimsy. One of the largest Ellwoods, built in a chic Beverly Hills area, later had its slender frame encased in Doric columns. Koenig, who never sought to make the ultimate statement, often organised his plans with bedrooms or living rooms in separate wings. He did, however, succeed in putting together just about the ultimate steel frame, but it was frustrating. The building trades, dominated by the carpenters who couldn't get used to the fine tolerances required in steel construction, caused the abandonment of the steel house program. Industry also proved uninterested in mass-producing these prototypes.

In its last years the success of the program was so great that there seemed a chance to build a whole innovative tract. A Quincy Jones and Frederick Emmons planned to make lots small, using the ground saved as a Green Belt. More unusual, the whole thing would not mar the landscape.

Unfortunately, the bureaucracy would not approve the small lots.

Toward the end, the old social message was coming through only faintly. Killingsworth, Brady and Smith's 'Triad', built in the posh coastal town of La Jolla, was a suave rehash of Miesian and Neutrian motives. The only innovation was a pioneering use of what Charles Jencks calls the LA Door. The Bourgeoisie had had the last word.

1635 Woods Drive, LA. Pierre Koenig, architect

1635 Woods Drive, LA. Pierre Koenig, architect

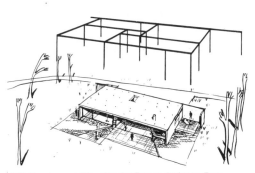

201 Chautauqua Way, Charles Eames designer, Eero Saarinen architect

Project 1945, Richard Neutra

82 Rivo Alto Canal, Long Beach, Killingsworth Brady and Smith

9036 Wonderland Park Avenue, LA, Pierre Koenig

Eichler House 1961, Quincy Jones and Frederick E Emmons (Perspective drawing: Kaz Nomura)

13187 Chalon Road West, LA, Wurster, Bernardi and Emmons

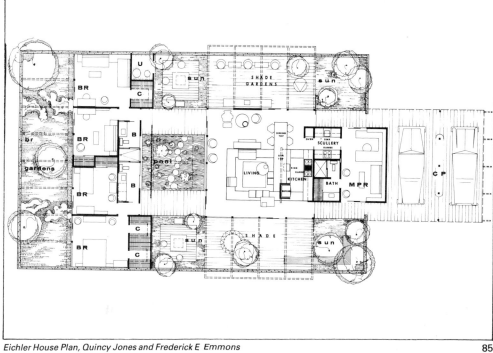

Eichler House Plan, Quincy Jones and Frederick E Emmons

85

Exterior, Killingsworth Brady and Smith, Triad Development, La Jolla

Interior, Eames and Saarinen

634, North Deerfield Avenue, San Gabriel, Thornton Abell

La Canada, Davidson

Pacific Palisades, Raphael Soriano

Pacific Palisades, Richard Neutra

Pasadena, Kemper Nomland

1129 Miradero Road, Beverly Hills, Craig Ellwood

Hidden Valley Road, Beverly Hills, Craig Ellwood

House 8, Killingsworth Brady and Smith

Arthur Golding
THE BIG OFFICES

In Los Angeles, six large architectural firms have had a strong impact on the man-made landscape. The six, Becket, DMJM, Gruen, Luckman, Martin and Pereira, all based in Los Angeles, continue to do significant work in Southern California. The following pages present a brief profile of each firm with a sampling of past projects.

The growth of large architectural, planning and engineering offices in Los Angeles is a postwar phenomenon. World War II and its aftermath brought a burst of population growth to the city, and with it a rapid pace of building. In response, three of the six firms discussed in this article were founded between 1945 and 1950, and the other three made major changes in structure and size during that same period.

Everything was new in 1945. There were no prototypes. The architects had to invent what they designed and they had to invent how to construct it. The frenetic building activity of those years gave the firms who learned to cope with it a special kind of experience and perspective. They were competent and efficient because they had to be, they were nearly always pragmatic because their clients were, and they were fearless: they could design anything.

Perhaps as a result of the postwar situation, the big Los Angeles firms emerged by the mid 1960s as generalists. They had designed hundreds of projects and seen enough built to call on a very broad experience. Schools, concert halls (Becket's Music Center), hospitals, apartments, museums, entire new universities (Pereira's University of California at Irvine), hotels, department stores, sports facilities (Luckman's Forum), shopping centres, research facilities, manufacturing plants, and of course, office buildings, had all been developed under their direction. A view of the downtown LA skyline shows the imprint of the large firms. A Wilshire Boulevard elevation would similarly demonstrate their presence.

Los Angeles, although it is now the second largest metropolis in the United States, is still very young as a city, almost formless, open. The built fabric is mostly first building and most of that is expendable. The physical setting is a great plain, a basin, with the expanse of the desert to the east and the Pacific to the west. The social structure is remarkably open for a major city. There are no old families, no really major concentrations of power. Institutions are young and evolving. In this context, change has become a norm. Yet the city is not without traditions, even in building. Some of them, rich and provocative in both root and branch, are discussed elsewhere in this issue. But the dominant tradition in LA is what Harold Rosenberg called, in another context, the tradition of the new.

Architecture in New York is taste and conservative development. In Chicago it is refinement of a solid tradition. In Los Angeles it is open experimentation. The big firms do this in a big way. It leads to spectacular successes

HOW BIG

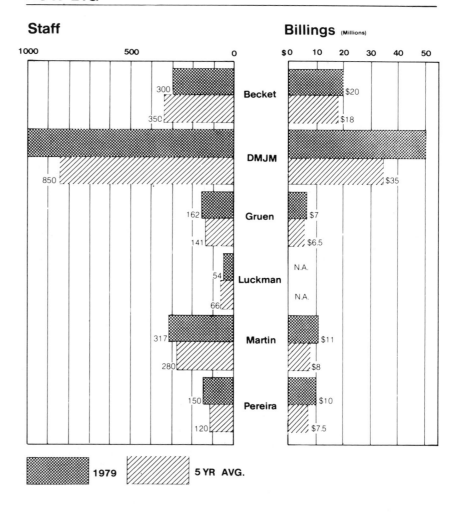

Staff

Billings (Millions)

and laughable failures. The tradition of the new requires a restless search for new forms, new attitudes, new ways of seeing. It leads to a fascination with technical innovation. The designers, the production architects, the managers, the consulting engineers, even the vendors and the contractors expect to find a different and maybe better way to do it each time. Not to start over, not to invent the wheel, but to look for incremental growth, a new technique, a new material, a new process – mirror glass, structural silicone, thin-shell precast, fibre-reinforced concrete ...

The strength of the big LA firms has been their capability, their ability to solve the problem, to make the thing work, to get it built. The design of facilities, rather than the making of architecture, has been their primary focus. When buildings are seen as facilities, as tools, they must above all be made to work. The design problem, mundane or exotic, must be stated clearly and solved. The key question, at all scales, is 'how does it work?' The bulk of time, energy and intelligence in the big LA offices has always been given to resolving this issue. The resulting process has reduced the

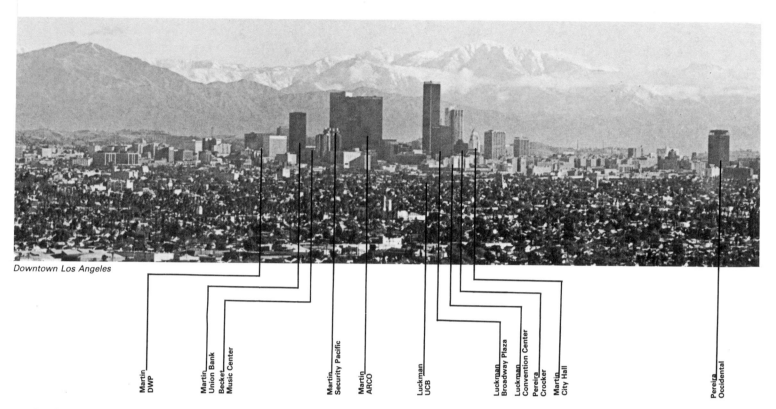

Downtown Los Angeles

Martin DWP
Martin Union Bank
Becket Music Center
Martin Security Pacific
Martin ARCO
Luckman UCB
Luckman Broadway Plaza
Luckman Convention Center
Pereira Crocker
Martin City Hall
Pereira Occidental

practice of architecture to two unequal components, problem solving and design. Design, in this context, is merely styling applied over a pragmatic armature of planning and construction. The styling has frequently been naive and trivial, but the underlying armature, more often than not, has been of a higher quality.

The experimentation and the experience of the big LA firms, the emphasis on technology not as an aesthetic issue but as a practical one, have led to a high level of competence and to a real pride in performance – the performance of the professional team and the performance of the finished building. Los Angeles International Airport (LAX), a product of the collaboration of Pereira and Luckman with Welton Becket and Associates and Paul Williams, is an exemplary LA design. Simple, efficient and flexible in plan, the airport facility required a relatively minor investment for infrastructure. A single one-way loop road provides access to parking on the inside (at first all on surface,

now nearly all in structures) and to linear one-storey terminal buildings on the outside. The terminals, which house ticketing and baggage handling, are linked below grade to satellite buildings that provide gate positions for aircraft.

LAX works. Its simple organisational system has allowed the airport to accept rapid growth in traffic and change in aircraft, including the introduction of the jumbo jets. Contrast the many US airports that have been forced to undergo a radical restructuring since 1960 (O'Hare, Newark), or the chaos of New York's JFK, or the monumental overdesign of D/FW. LAX is elaborately crowned with an absurd jewel of 1950s exuberance: the theme tower and restaurant. This folly, a vision of the future as it looked then, is certain to be designated an historical landmark before the end of the century.

With the maturing of their original founders in the late 1960s, each of the big LA firms has come to face the major issue of transition to a new structure. Some have passed this point successfully, while others are now engaged in the process. The founders are no longer active at Becket and Gruen, and only one of the four remains at DMJM.

The new principals in all the big firms are professionals, most of them architects, a few engineers. They often come from a background in project management, and they are more specialised in their experience than were the founders. Few of the designers in the big firms are the principals, and few of the principals are designers. An exception to this pattern was set in motion in 1964 when Cesar Pelli and A J Lumsden joined DMJM, Pelli as director of design, Lumsden as his assistant. After four years at DMJM, Pelli joined Gruen Associates as Partner for Design. He was active as a Gruen principal until 1977, when he left the firm to become Dean of the Yale School of Architecture. Lumsden took over the design responsibility at DMJM, and later became a principal in that firm.

Engineering is the largest component of DMJM's billings, but architecture has been a significant element of the firm's practice since 1964, under Pelli and Lumsden. Their early collaboration produced two extraordinary designs that have had a very wide influence in Los Angeles and elsewhere, Sunset Mountain Park and FAA. Mountain Park, the groundscraper apartment complex that stepped down

a hillside in a densely organised and highly sculptural form, was never built. The FAA office building, in which a taut membrane of mirror glass and aluminum is wrapped over and under and around the building, defining it as a fragile volume, was delayed some five years between design and construction. As built, it is the clearest LA statement of the ideal of technological romanticism.

First Pelli at Gruen and now Lumsden at DMJM provide models of a new direction for the big LA firms. The competence, professionalism and pragmatism of the big office is joined with a new sophistication and a new standard of excellence. Much has been made of the slick LA style of skin buildings sometimes practised by both men, but their greater influence may ultimately lie in the precedent they have set in the big LA offices and in the pattern of working with the strengths of those offices to make architecture.

Urban Nucleus project for Sunset Mountain Park near Los Angeles. Designed under the direction of Cesar Pelli, Director of Design, DMJM 1964–68

Los Angeles International Airport 1955–61. Pereira & Luckman, Becket, with Paul Williams. Master Plan by William L Pereira Associates, 1967

Reunion, Dallas. 1000 room hotel and 50-storey theme tower, 1978.

BECKET

WELTON BECKET ASSOCIATES, ARCHITECTS AND EN-GINEERS

Principal Office
Los Angeles

Other Offices
Chicago, New York, San Francisco, Houston, Atlanta

Services
Planning, Architecture, Interior Design, Graphics, Engineering (Structural, Mechanical, Electrical)

Size of Staff
1979 Personnel: 300 (80% professional)
5-year average: 350 (79% professional)

Volume of Work
1979 Billings: $20 million
5-year average: $18 million

Geographical Distribution of Work
Southern California: 25% 1979, 20% 5-year average
Other US: 55% 1979, 65% 5-year average
International: 20% 1979, 15% 5-year average

Principals
MacDonald Becket, FAIA, President; Alan Rosen; Henry Brennan; George Hammond

Capsule History
Founded 1933 by Welton Becket. Plummer, Wurdeman and Becket, 1933. Wurdeman and Becket, 1939. Welton Becket and Associates, 1949–

Music Center, Los Angeles, 1964.

Prudential Square, Los Angeles, 1949

Century City, master plan, 1959–64

Pan Pacific Auditorium, Los Angeles, 1935

Los Angeles Memorial Sports Arena, 1960.

Bullock's Pasadena, 1947

DMJM

DANIEL, MANN, JOHNSON & MENDENHALL

Planning Architecture Engineering Systems Economics

Principal Office
Los Angeles

Other Offices
Anchorage, Baltimore, Denver, Honolulu, Houston, Las Vegas, New Orleans, Portland (Oregon), Redwood City, Washington. Other US Branch offices: 17. Overseas offices: 8.

Services
Planning, Architecture, Interior Design, Engineering (Civil, Structural, Mechanical, Electrical, Hydraulic, Traffic), Transportation Planning, Acoustics, Lighting Design, Construction Management, Economics, Land Development, Systems Analysis.

Size of Staff
1979 Personnel: 1000 (62% professional)
5-year average: 850 (58% professional)

Volume of Work
1979 Billings: $50 million
5-year average: $35 million

Geographical Distribution of Work
Southern California: 20% 1979, 20% 5-year average
Other US: 35% 1979, 30% 5-year average
International: 45% 1979, 50% 5-year average

Principals
Albert A Dorman, President, Chief Executive Office; Irvan F Mendenhall, Chairman of the Board; Stanley M Smith, Sven B Svendsen, Marvin J Kudroff, Anthony J Lumsden (partial listing)

Capsule History
Founded 1946 by Philip J Daniel, Arthur E Mann, S Kenneth Johnson and Irvan F Mendenhall. Daniel, Mann, Johnson & Mendenhall, 1946—

Federal Aviation Administration, Hawthorn, aluminium and mirror glass cladding, 1975

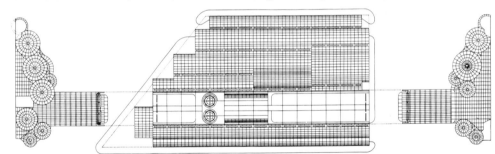

Proposed Hotel, Beverly Hills, 440 rooms, 1973

Marina City, Marina del Rey, 1975

One Park Plaza, Los Angeles, 1971

Manufacturers' Trust, Beverly Hills, 1974

91

GRUEN

GRUEN ASSOCIATES
Architecture Planning Engineering

Principal Office
Los Angeles

Other Offices
New York, Washington

Services
Planning, Architecture, Interior Design, Graphics, Engineering (Civil, Structural), Traffic and Transportation Planning

Size of Staff
1979 Personnel: 162 (85% professional)
5-year average: 141 (85% professional)

Volume of Work
1979 Billings: $7 million
5-year average: $6.5 million

Geographical Distribution of Work
Southern California: 30% 1979, 40% 5-year average
Other US: 60% 1979, 50% 5-year average
International: 10% 1979, 10% 5-year average

Principals
Dan M Branigan, AIA; William H Dahl, AIA; Herman Guttman, AIA; Abbott Harle, AIA, ASID; Ki Suh Park, AIA, AICP; Allen M Rubenstein, ASCE; Ben H Southland, AIA, AICP; Beda Zwicker, AIA

Capsule History
Founded 1945 by Victor Gruen. Gruen and Krummeck, 1945. Victor Gruen Associates, 1951, Gruen Associates, 1968–

Winter Garden, Niagara Falls, 1978. Steel frame, glass curtain wall

San Bernardino, aerial view, 1963–74.

San Bernardino City Hall, 1974.

Valencia. View of a pedestrian paseo, 1965.

Pacific Design Center, Los Angeles, 1975.

2-19-78

Marina del Rey, master planning, 1959.

LUCKMAN

THE LUCKMAN PARTNERSHIP, INC.

Planning Architecture Engineering

Principal Office

Los Angeles

Services

Planning, Architecture, Space Planning, Construction Management, Economics

Size of Staff

1979 Personnel: 54 (83% professional)

5-year average: 66 (86% professional)

Volume of Work

1979 Billings: not available

5-year average: not available

Geographical Distribution of Work:

Southern California: 58% 1979, 45% 5-year average

Other US: 42% 1979, 55% 5-year average

International: 0% 1979, 0% 5-year average

Principals

Charles Luckman FAIA; James M Luckman, AIA; Edward R Jones, Jr AIA; Richard C Niblack, AIA

Capsule History

Founded 1950 by William L Pereira and Charles Luckman (see Pereira). Pereira & Luckman, 1950. Charles Luckman Associates, 1958. Subsidiary of Ogden Corporation, 1968. The Luckman Partnership, Inc 1977–

Aloha Stadium, Honolulu, 1975.

Los Angeles Zoo, 1966.

Los Angeles Convention and Exhibition Center, 1971.

Broadway Plaza Los Angeles, 1974

Theme building and restaurant, L A Airport, 1955–61.

Marineland of the Pacific. Pereira & Luckman

The Forum, Inglewood, 1967.

93

ARCO, Atlantic Richfield Plaza, Los Angeles, 1973.

MARTIN
ALBERT C MARTIN AND ASSOCIATES
Planning Architecture Engineering
Principal Office
Los Angeles
Other Offices
Irvine Ca, Houston, New York
Services
Planning, Architecture, Interior Design, Graphics, Engineering (Civil, Structural, Mechanical, Electrical), Cost Estimating
Size of Staff
1979 Personnel: 317 (77% professional)
5-year average: 280 (80% professional)
Volume of Work
1979 Billings: $11 million
5-year average: $8 million
Geographical Distribution of Work
Southern California: 90% 1979, 10% 5-year average
Other US: 10% 1979, 10% 5-year average
International: 0% 1979, 0% 5-year average
Principals
Albert C Martin, Jr; J Edward Martin
Capsule History
Founded 1906 by Albert C Martin Sr. Albert C Martin, 1906. Albert C Martin and Associates, 1945–

Security Pacific World Headquarters, 1975.

May Company, Fairfax and Wilshire, 1939.

St Vincent's Church, Los Angeles, 1923

Department of Water and Power, 1965.

Los Angeles City Hall, 1929.

PEREIRA

WILLIAM L PEREIRA ASSOCIATES
Planners Architects Engineers

Principal Office
Los Angeles

Other Offices
Corona del Mar, Ca

Services
Planning, Architecture, Interior Design, Graphics

Size of Staff
1979 Personnel: 150 (80% professional)
5-year average: 120 (80% professional)

Volume of Work
1979 Billings: $10 million
5-year average: $7.5 million

Geographical Distribution of Work
Southern California: 48% 1979, 35% 5-year average
Other US: 25% 1979, 15% 5-year average
International: 27% 1979, 50% 5-year average

Principals
William L Pereira, FAIA, Chairman and President; Neil W
Birnbrauer, Jack Kassel, Roy G Schmidt

Capsule History
Founded 1931 by William L Pereira. Pereira & Pereira,
1931. William L Pereira and Associates, 1945. Pereira &
Luckman and Associates, 1950. William L Pereira Associates, 1958–

Transamerica Pyramid, San Francisco, 1972.

Los Angeles County Museum of Art, 1965

Irvine Ranch Master Plan. 93,000 acres. 1960

Los Angeles County Museum of Art, 1965.

Times Mirror Building, Los Angeles, 1973

Union Oil Center, Los Angeles, 1958.

CBS Television City, Hollywood, 1952.

John V Mutlow
ARCHITECTURE IN LA TODAY

The trip to Los Angeles was long and came about almost by accident. It started in London in 1967 as a desire to visit the States. The boat trip from Southampton to New York was uneventful, but the anticipation of seeing New York slowly overcame me, and I was not disappointed. Cultural shock had begun. It is impossible to imagine the intensity of density of block upon block of skyscrapers.

A five-day, five-night Greyhound bus trip from New York, with brief stops at Montreal Expo and Chicago, and 4000 miles of everchanging landscapes ensued before my arrival in downtown Los Angeles. There is something wrong with bus stations. They never appear to be entry points, always departure points with their drab and dreary architecture. But a short while later, after a 15-mile trip by bus along the Wilshire corridor on the always underrated LA transit system, I knew I had arrived. A linear zone stretched from a downtown then void of skyscrapers along a high intensity corridor to the Pacific Ocean at Santa Monica.

Graduate studies at UCLA concentrated on 'Scenarios of the Future', and resulted in a close relationship with the aerospace industry, forecasting the future to the year 2000 with TRW (utilising Olaf Helmer's and Ted Gordon's delphi technique), the Jet Propulsion Laboratory's Lunar Landing Vehicle, and Hughes Aircraft. Simulation chambers of the aerospace industry extend the human thought and perception processes, and the concentration of minds at the human 'think tanks' of the Rand Corporation and SDC (Systems Development Corporation) researches the untried. Universal Studios recreate the imagery of Hollywood and the stars, and Disneyland makes believe that everything and everyone is wonderful and real.

There is no history or culture in the traditional sense of the word, but simply the culture of the present and the history of the future, a history that is carried on today with the flights of the space shuttle 'Enterprise,' piggybacking a Boeing 747 based in the desert at Edwards Air Force Base. For a European who had been steeped in the culture of history, this was difficult to perceive, let alone assimilate. But as time passes, the realisation that this is frontierland comes home. Vast open spaces, deserts, mountains and the low-intensity urban fabric become a part of life, and the linkage between the parts is the freeway, the freeway that links suburban wonderland with air-conditioned indoor shopping centres, airports with subterranean garages, hospitals with Forest Lawn mortuaries.

This is the typology for architecture in Los Angeles, a theatrical scenic backdrop, a city of stage sets – stages that can be set by the architect. Once one has become oriented to the urban lifestyle of Los Angeles, architecture begins to assume a different meaning. A 'blue whale' adjacent to Spanish colonial houses, taut skin on a government office building, a mirror building gently sited in a park, houses assembled with component parts, a Miesian art college or a high art interior for attorneys: they are all stage sets, an integral and essential part of the Los Angeles scenery.

Stage Set – Taut Skin Membrane. On arriving in Los Angeles today, one heads immediately for the 'blue whale' (Pacific Design Centre), designed by Cesar Pelli of Gruen Associates. Aptly suited to its tenants and clientele, interior furnishing suppliers, its status as a landmark has preceded it. In 1967 that honour also went to the Teledyne Laboratories, a high-tech building, more sensitive to its surroundings, designed by Cesar Pelli and Tony Lumsden at DMJM.

This type of architecture, a standard structural system with a rhythmic technologic membrane, received international recognition with the curtain wall of Lever House. Now more refined, more varied, and more responsive to the climate as well as to technological advances, the continued evolution of this stage set, especially by Anthony J Lumsden, is clearly expressed in the crisp enclosure of the Federal Aviation Administration's Office Building, in the aluminium sandwich panel of the Linder Plaza, and in the stainless steel, reflective skin of the Fluor Corporation.

Stage Set – Miesian. This rational and highly organised set has most recently returned to the forefront with John Entenza's case study homes in the 1950s and early 1960s, the Art Centre College by Craig Ellwood spanning a valley in Pasadena, the flexible moment resistant structural system of the Parker Hannifin Aerospace Complex by A C Martin, and the Helmut Schulitz residence in the Hollywood Hills. The Miesian philosophy and structural hierarchy is apparent, with exposed structural steel columns and beams clearly articulated, and infill panels of steel or glass recessed and less dominant.

Community Participation. Upon graduating from the futures programme of UCLA, an extended involvement with local social history ensued with the Pico Union Community, a Mexican and Latin American community determined to have a say in its own future. Low-income families and senior citizens were involved in the design of their own community-owned housing.

Stage Set – Modern. This period was enhanced by rationalistic modern architecture that, even if somewhat conservative for Los Angeles, has set a stage for quality: Dan Dworsky's Cerritos College, and later the Plaza, a low-rise office building in downtown Los Angeles; Pulliam Matthews' Student Union for the California Polytechnic College at Pomona; and Quincy Jones' (a pioneer of tract homes in the 1950s) design for the Warner Office Building (music records) in Burbank.

Stage Set – Historical Illusion. A true illusion of the past, a recreated ancient Roman villa of the Papyri: the illusion was the desire of J Paul Getty for an art museum at his palatial estate in Pacific Palisades, designed by Langdon and Wilson. The villa is complete with extensive interiors and landscaped gardens by Emmet Wemple.

Stage Set – High Art. The appropriateness of architecture as high art in Los Angeles has produced a serious form that combines architecture with art, playfulness, exuberance, warmth, and celebration, and is typified by the mastery over form of both Charles Moore and Frank Gehry. Here, the full artistic potential of the low-tech system is realised with multi-faceted, non-loadbearing walls of various sizes and shapes, defining spaces both vertically and horizontally. The quality and softness of light as it falls on surfaces of pastel shades and numerous tones, and more recently, the introduction of unfamiliar space-defining elements of chain link fence, sono tubes, and flowing curtains, have added to the awareness and understanding of space, and have reinforced the stage set environment. This set is uniquely suited to the hot, dry climate of Southern California. The structure is wood balloon framing and the wall finish is stucco. It typifies today just as the Mediterranean style typified the 1930s and 1940s.

Stage Set – Hollywood Modern. The lavishness and exuberance of the Hollywood metaphors of the past, with their elements of monumental scale, complexity of structure, gaiety, variation of spatial interrelationships, and continuous movement of water have been re-interpreted in the six-storey atrium of the Bonaventure Hotel by John Portman.

Stage Set – New Directions. After joining the architectural faculty at USC in 1975, new relationships and directions were formed and my horizons began to expand. Several of the new directions in architecture are stemming from the younger faculty who teach at the local universities and colleges, experimenting with and stretching the architectural foundations of Los Angeles.

Stage Set – Component Parts. The California version of high-tech architecture, utilising off-the-shelf component parts of wood, steel, and aluminium trusses, steel columns and staircases, asbestos or steel siding or decking and aluminium shop front curtain walls – the whole assembled into architecture – is typified by the de Bretteville residence in the Hollywood Hills.

Stage Set – Drawings as Art Form. Exquisite drawings or models, more than any other media, typify the strengths of architectural expression, and owe much to the magnificent drawings for the Hollywood film and stage sets of yesterday. Architecture is transformed in the paintings of Roland Coate and Craig Ellwood, the graphic drawings of Coy Howard, the pencil drawings of Frank Dimster, and the seductively elegant models of Eric Moss and Jim Stafford: here is surely an art unto itself.

Stage Set – Stage Set. Here the stage set is complete. The architect, as stage set designer, provides immediate impressions of space-defining elements to millions of viewers in an art that was practised with acclaim by Bill Pereira and now by Craig Hodgetts, representing the true meeting of architecture and Hollywood in Los Angeles.

And standing slightly aside, yet not apart, from this series of events are the indisputable gurus of the Los Angeles architectural scene, Charles and Ray Eames. The classic Herman Miller chairs and the exquisite beauty of their short documentary films are part of a fortune of talent that has had international impact and still carries on after Charles' untimely death.

Conclusion. Hollywood could not exist without the cinema, the stage, and the scenery. The film backlots are disappearing, and the stage sets are now the streets and urban fabric of LA. Seasons do not exist. Time is the present. The light is bright, the use of colour varied and intense. The freedom that stage scenery implies allows a variety of alternative directions to develop whilst the step-by-step logic and methodology of the aerospace industry supports the rationale of the high-tech. These apparent oppositions combined with the absence of historical culture have promulgated a variety of architectural directions. A unique 'sense of place' owes its culture to the Hollywood of the Thirties and the Disney of the Sixties. Los Angeles is a magnet, and once you comprehend it, you will feel as Ron Herron did, overheard quoting the Eagles' 'Hotel California' as he stepped onto a Lockheed 1011 at LAX after his yearly sojourn in Los Angeles, *'You can check out any time you like, but you will never leave.'*

Federal Aviation Building, DMJM

Offices, Luckman

Art Centre, Ellwood/Tyler

Pacific Design Center, Pelli/Gruen

Bonaventure, Portman

Teledyne, DMJM

Willow Glen House, de Bretteville

Green Machine, Glen Small

Warehouse, Eric Moss

Senior Citizen Housing, John Mutlow

Schulitz House

Bahamas Housing, Dimster

Charles Moore

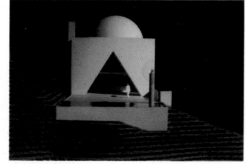

Rowland Coate

Law Office, Gehry

STAGE SET— TAUT SKIN MEMBRANE

Best Model, DMJM (Lumsden)

Teledyne Interior, DMJM

Century Plaza, DMJM

Pacific Design Centre, Detail, Gruen (Pelli)

Pacific Design Centre, Gruen (Pelli)

Reflections, Pacific Design Centre, Gruen (Pelli)

Luckman Office Building (Ocean Gate)

Manufacturers' Bank, DMJM (Lumsden)

One Park Plaza, DMJM (Lumsden)

Linder Plaza Office, Reibsamen Nickels Rex

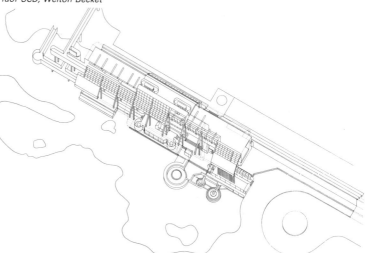
Fluor SCD, Welton Becket

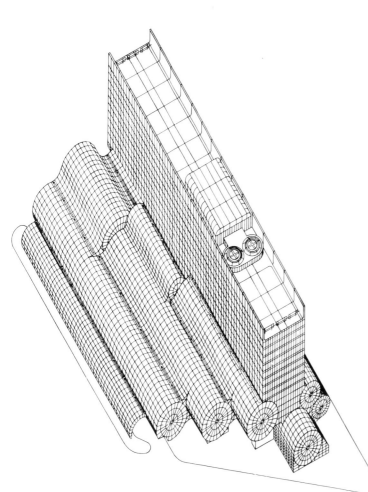
Beverly Hills Hotel, DMJM (Lumsden)

SWRP, DMJM (Lumsden)

Bumi Daya Bank, DMJM (Lumsden)

Interior, Pacific Design Center, Gruen (Pelli)

STAGE SET—
MODERN

Warner Brothers Records, A Quincy Jones

Annenberg Center, USC, A Quincy Jones

S W College, Reibsamen Nickels & Rex

Union Oil Research Center, William L Pereira Associates

University Station, DMJM

University Station, DMJM

Cal Poly Student Union, Pulliam Matthews

Lomax Residence, Lomax Hills Associates

W College, Reibsamen Nickels & Rex

Theater Arts Building, Dworsky

Herald Mail Newspaper Plant, William L Periera Associates

Cerritos College Auto Technology Center, William L Periera Associates

South West College, Reibsamen Nickels & Rex

South West College, Reibsamen Nickels & Rex

Theatre, Dworsky

Theatre, landscape detail, Dworsky

Theater Arts Building, California State University, Dworsky

103

STAGE SET—
HISTORIC ILLUSION

J Paul Getty Museum. Architects—Langdon & Wilson. Landscape—Emmet L Wemple & Associates

Basilica of Cybele

Statue of Heracles

Herculaneum goes to Malibu

Interior, general view

Atrium view

West Porch

HERACULANEUM GOES TO MALIBU

The J Paul Getty Museum displays a quality of construction and landscaping so perfect that it is breathtaking. It is also bizarre to know that the same architects were responsible for another Los Angeles monument—the C & A Building. Though one can question the relevance of importing a re-created Roman Villa from Heraculaneum to Malibu, one is still astonished to find that craftsmanship of this standard is still possible.

Hall of Marbles

The C & A Building

STAGE SET—
HIGH ART

FRANK GEHRY

Gehry House

Gehry House, yard

Law Office, interior

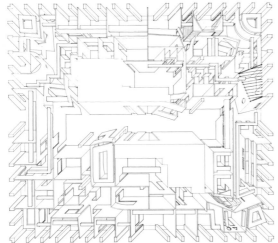

Berger Berger Kahn Shafton & Moss Law Offices

Law Office, interior

Gehry House, kitchen

CHARLES MOORE

Moore, layering

Burns House

Moore, playing

Moore, interior

Burns House, Inner Court

Moore cornering

Entrance hall

Moore layering

Moore Facade Detail

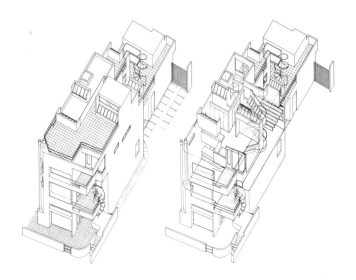

Diamond Beach Residence, Mutlow

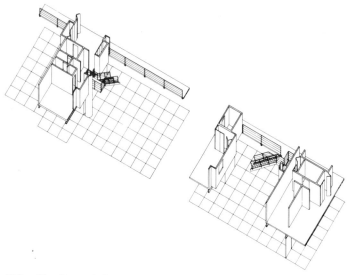

Willow Glen House, de Bretteville

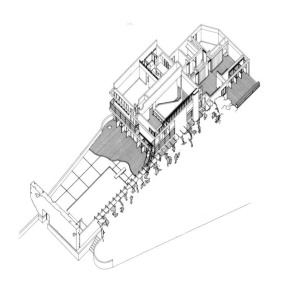

Chuck Lagreco Residence

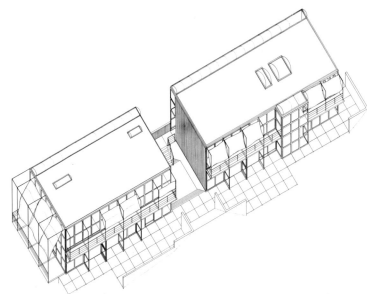

Willow Glen House, de Bretteville

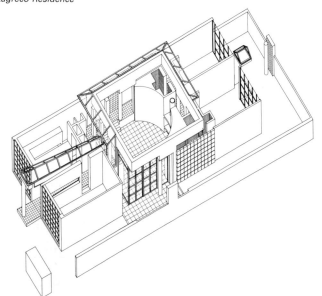

Ensenada House, Mexico, Morphosis

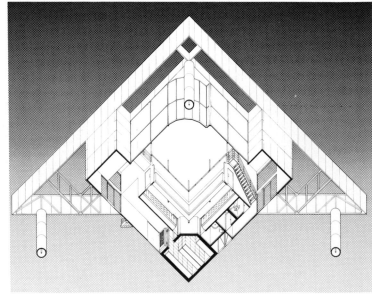

World Savings & Loan, Cerritos Camnitzer Cotton & Vreeland

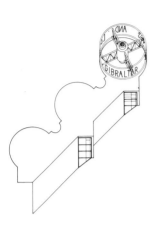

Schmidt Residence, Malibu, Ed Niles

Schmidt Residence, Malibu, Ed Niles

Gibraltar Bank, Moss Stafford

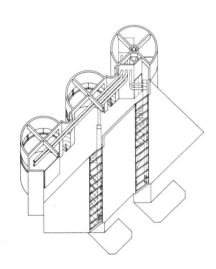

Gibraltar Bank, Moss Stafford

Schmidt Residence, plans

Villa Scalabrina, Panos Koulermos

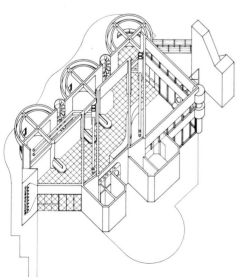

Gibraltar Bank, Moss Stafford

Nilson Residence, Eugene Kupper

STAGE SET—
HOLLYWOOD

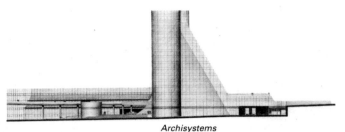

Archisystems

Pasadena Retail Centre, Kober Associates

16000 Ventura Boulevard, Kober Associates

Archisystems, proposed Bunker Hill Hotel

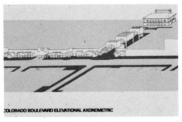

COLORADO BOULEVARD ELEVATIONAL AXONOMETRIC

Pasadena Retail Centre, Kober Associates

Elrod House, Palm Springs, John Lautner

Stevens House, Malibu, Lautner

Stevens House, Malibu, Lautner

Bonaventure Hotel, John Portman

Facade at sunset, John Portman

Interior, Bonaventure

STAGE SET—NEW DIRECTIONS

Playa Del Ray Duplex.
Eric Moss and James Stafford

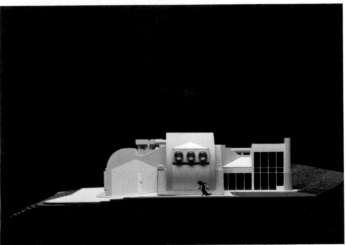

Pin Ball House, LA. Eric Moss and James Stafford

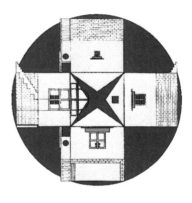

Tee Shirt House. Morphosis

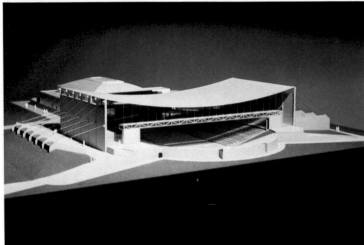

Loyola, Marymont Pavilion. Ray Kappe

Water Treatment Plant. Ray Kappe

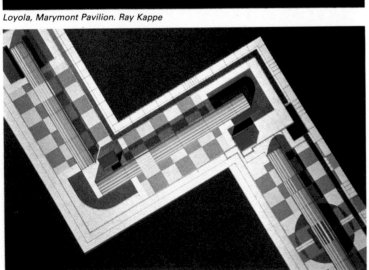

The Promenade, Bunker Hill. Kamnitzer Cotton Vreeland

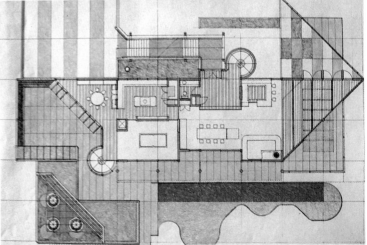

House Plan. Frank Dimster

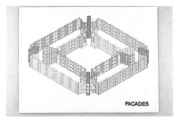

Facades, Pico Union Plaza. John Mutlow

Pico Union Plaza. John Mutlow

'Pico Union Plaza. John Mutlow

Dohramann Company. Morphosis

Willow Glen House. De Bretteville

Willow Glen House. De Bretteville

House at Malibu. Ed Niles

Delma House. Morphosis

Trailer Pad. Green Machine, Glen Small House. Frank Dimster

Portable Crane. Green Machine, Glen Small

Johnson Residence. Chris Dawson

115

STAGE SET—MIESIAN

Schulitz House

Corner detail

Interior detail

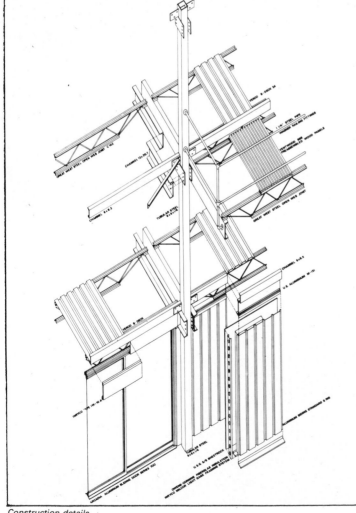

Construction details

Interior

Art Centre, gallery with atrium

Art Centre College of Design. Ellwood and Tyler

Bank of America. Tyler and Wooley

Art Centre College of Design. Ellwood and Tyler

Parker Hannifin. A C Martin

URO Office Building. Tyler and Wooley

Parker Hannifin. A C Martin

URO Office Interior. Tyler and Wooley

117

STAGE SET— DRAWINGS

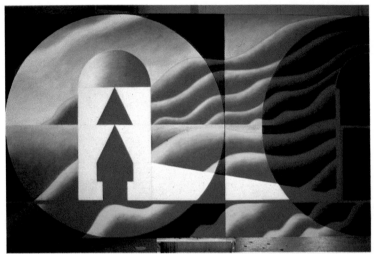

Painting. Roland Coate

Alexander House, Montecito. Roland Coate

Hollywood House. Roland Coate

Drawing by Coy Howard

Yellow House Painting. Roland Coate

Drawing by Coy Howard

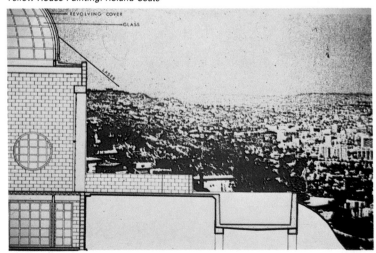

Leland House, Lazer. Roland Coate

Leland House, Elevations. Roland Coate

Drawing by Coy Howard

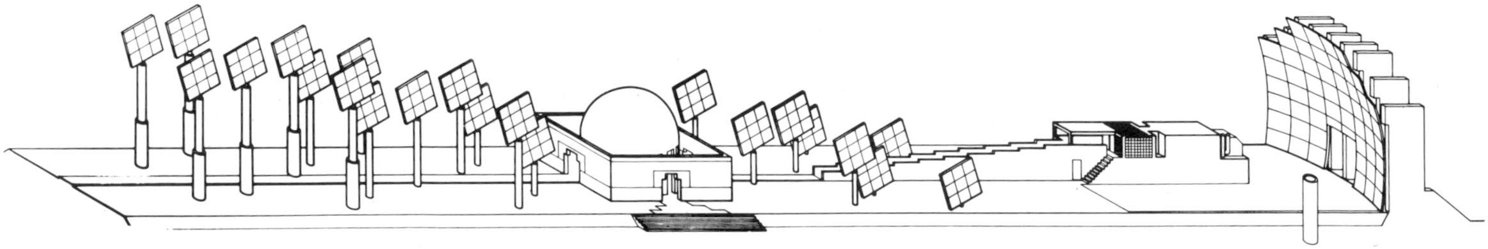

Solar Crematorium. Frederick Fisher

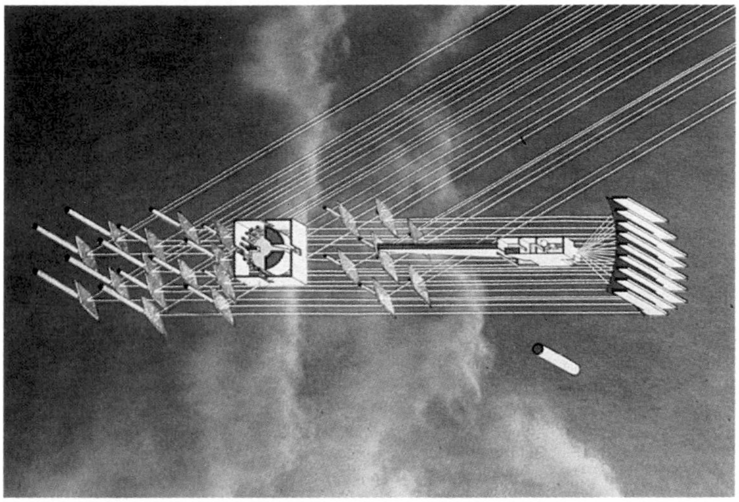

Solar Crematorium. Frederick Fisher

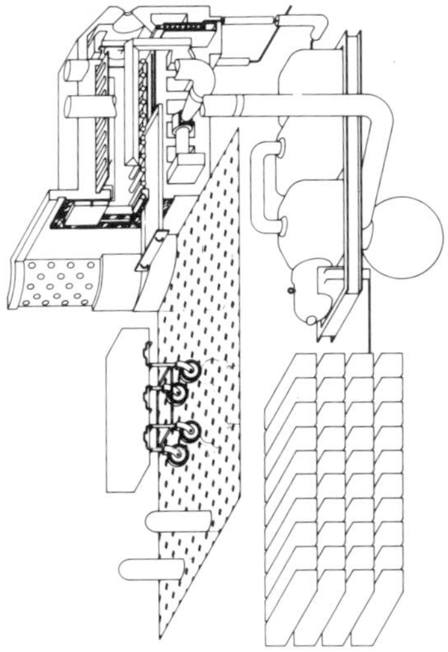

Solar Crematorium. Frederick Fisher

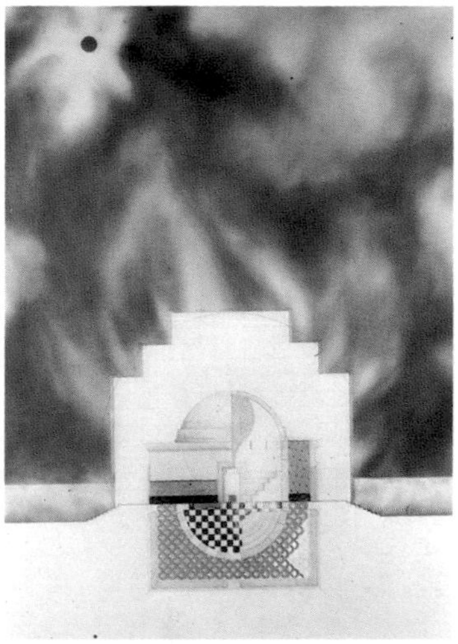

Solar Crematorium. Frederick Fisher

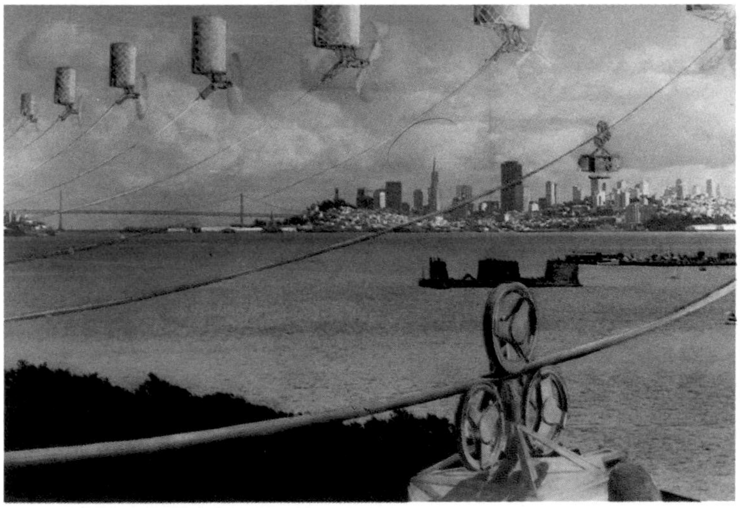

Stage Set. Craig Hodgetts

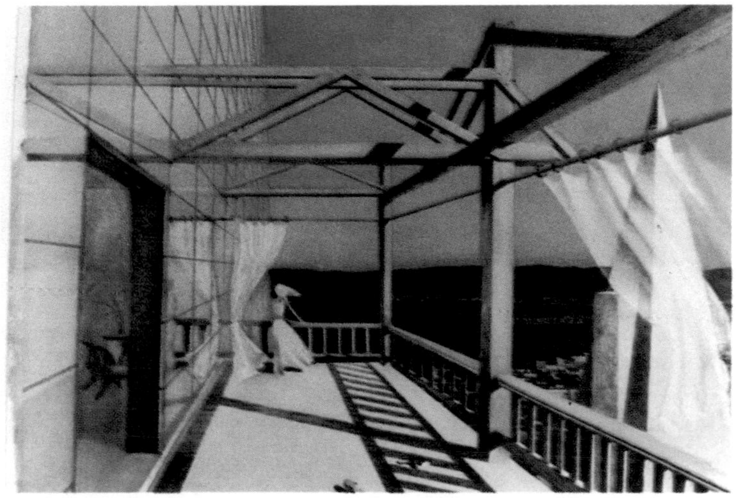

Stage Set. Craig Hodgetts

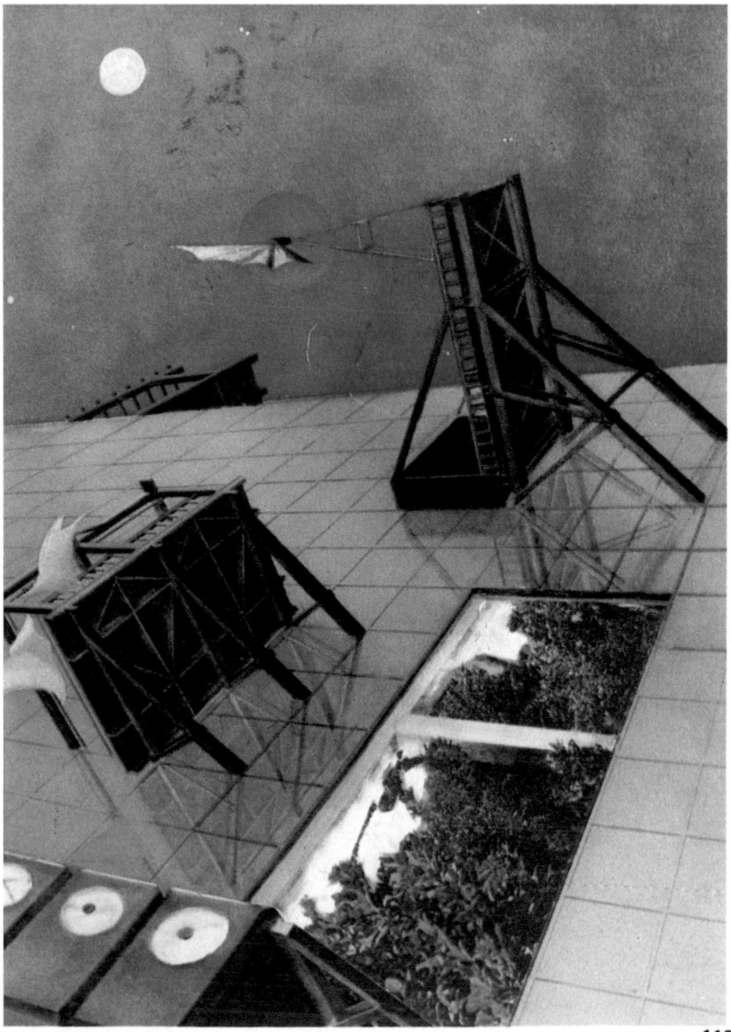

Stage Set. Craig Hodgetts

Chris Dawson

THE ICONOGRAPHY OF THE MUNDANE

AN ATTEMPT TO EXPLAIN THE ORDINARINESS OF AN EXTRAORDINARY PLACE

How does one convey to an audience (presumably uninitiated) the ordinary, the extraordinary, the extraordinary ordinariness and the ordinary extraordinariness of a city in which one lives and works? Can it be done without resorting to the hyperbole of the Banhams and Wolfes, or the *mea culpa* of the Plagens, or the pedantry, however eloquent, of a Carey McWilliams? The archetypal LA is no doubt that seen through the eyes of Raymond Chandler—the Eldorado of the 1930s, 1940s, and 1950s. Los Angeles is the grotesque genius child of the shocked, God-fearing, conservative parents of the American mid-west.

Everybody either loves LA or hates LA, and some people live in LA.

How does one describe any city? As an outsider, one notices only the extraordinary; as an insider, one is concerned with the ordinary. This essay is about the ordinary, since, after a decade of residence, I now consider myself an insider (maintaining admittedly more than a modicum of the outsider's naïve Eldorado vision). I cannot condemn LA as the monstrous progeny of Sodom and Gomorrah described by the breast-beaters, nor can I accept the 'fun and sun in the surf' image now so familiar to European audiences. The East Coast intellectual snobbism, currently spearheaded by Woody Allen (turning right on a red light is *indeed* a cultural advantage), is a similar aberration of both observation and justice. Los Angeles *is* provincial—unabashedly so—except among the (envious) culture vultures who view New York as the only source of salvation for their tax-deductible souls.

Los Angeles isn't any one of the things people say about it—it's *all* the things everyone says about it!

It seems to me that a personal view of any place is a series of images and vignettes, not a coherent, carefully ordered and inclusive academic argument. The selected images are just as fragmented as one's day-to-day life. They attempt to convey an iconology of the mundane as a daily theatre. These images are deliberately 'multiple'. If there *is* anything special about LA it is that there is so much of it—so much of everything. Charles Jencks' book *Daydream Houses of LA* conveys some correct but wrongly stated impressions. The book treats its subjects as unique, isolated objects—the extraordinary thing about LA is not simply that these houses exist, but that hundreds and thousands of them exist. This is true of almost all aspects of life here. The visuals *attempt* to convey this. These images try to show those things which may seem extraordinary to the visitor, but which are ordinary to the locals. The Banham/Wolfe attitude to LA is that of tourist, lover, sentimentalist; it isn't wrong, but it is distorted. If LA *is* Tinseltown (Hollywood), Sin City, Fun and Sun City, Money City, it is *also* true-blue, redneck, white-knuckled, and tight-fisted. In a similar vein, maybe 'pop' art is only art in a context of fine art: Campbell's soup cans are interesting in New York; a Velazquez is more interesting in LA.

Los Angeles is built advertising. The images one normally sees as examples of eccentricity (hot dogs, donuts, pianos, hats) are actually the natural result of a city which exists to sell. The commercial strips exist as physical entities only in their signs and billboards; the buildings serve merely as backdrops to the signs, not vice versa as is the case in any 'normal' place. Again, these phenomena become commonplace to the resident but seem eccentric to the visitor. In global terms they are unusual; locally they are not—which is not to say they are unappreciated.

Derek Walker's invitation to participate in this section brought a swift reflex: 'Oh no. Here we go again! An article on LA, in a British magazine, written and edited by a bunch of starry-eyed, gloating, expatriate Europeans, and appearing on the news stands in the dead of winter—there's no justice!' How *does* one explain—entertainingly—what it is like to live in an extraordinary place without being a sensationalist on the one hand or blasé and boring on the other. '*When a man is tired of London, he is tired of life,*' said Johnson. A man constantly excited by LA is either a journalist or a defective. Does a Parisian describe his life in terms of *haute couture* and *haute cuisine*? No, but this is not to say he does not appreciate these things and the beauty that surrounds him (even as he stands in line for the bus, sweats in the métro, and suffers cheap wine with his stew), but these things are not the essential elements of his daily life. So, too, surfing, Malibu and movie stars are not the essential elements of life in LA.

One way to describe life in a particular place is to point out differences between that place and the realm of the audience's experience. And I suppose the other way is to point out similarities. The following list of commonplace features of the city leaves the reader to decide which are familiar and which peculiar.

○ **Palm trees**
○ **Shops** (mostly supermarkets) open 24 hours—11–20 hours per day is normal
○ **Newspapers** are 90% advertisement
○ **Sun**—means never having to wear a coat
○ **Fast food**—decent, clean, ordinary food
○ **Density**—lack of it. It's changing
○ **Cars**—bigger but getting smaller—still surprising and delighting with extravagant paint jobs and fix-ups—essential to life
○ **Smog**—just got through ten straight days of breathing air which is actually harmful (and this with more controls than anywhere in the world)
○ **Parks**—not many of them
○ **Suburbs**—it's all suburbs
○ **Variety**—may be the spice of life, but too much will give you heartburn
○ **Signs** and utility poles—'*Go to hell, Peter Blake, it's great!*'
○ **The tacky, ugly and cheap**
○ **The rich, opulent and beautiful**

○ **Beaches**—they're beaches—not the South of France
○ **People** are more relaxed—try getting into a fancy restaurant without a jacket
○ **People** are too relaxed—go to a fancy restaurant and find yourself sitting next to a guy in a T-shirt and shorts
○ **Cars**—they're necessity: ordinary—they're a god: extraordinary
○ **Cars**—the driving is cooler (and better) than in Europe but getting worse
○ **Seasons**—it rains, and when it rains, *it rains*
○ **Snow** is for skiing on
○ **Disneyland** is great
○ **Radio**—4 million stations, all music
○ **TV**—24 hours
○ **Downtown**—must have been great in the 1930s—or was it?
○ **Malibu et al**—do you realise most writers have described only the west side of LA to you? The rest isn't worth describing. Suburbs-by-the-sea are great; otherwise not so great.
○ **Personalised license plates**—ego-trip for 25 dollars a year—most people have no taste, can't spell, lack wit
○ **Cars**—there must be more Porsches and Mercedes here than in Germany
○ **Buses**—quite plentiful
○ **Billboards**—LA is billboards—Getrude Stein ('*There's no there, there*') was absolutely wrong: there are too many theres there, which makes it difficult to describe and thus, for some, uncomfortable
○ **Comfort**—it's too comfortable here
○ **The rest of America** looks at southern California just as Europeans do—with a mixture of hate and envy
○ **Have a nice day!**

Bibliography

Reyner Banham, *Los Angeles, Four Ecologies*
Tom Wolfe, *General Essays*
Peter Plagens, 'Ecology of Evil', *Artforum Magazine*
Carey McWilliams, *An Island on the Land*
Charles Jencks, *Daydream Houses of Los Angeles*

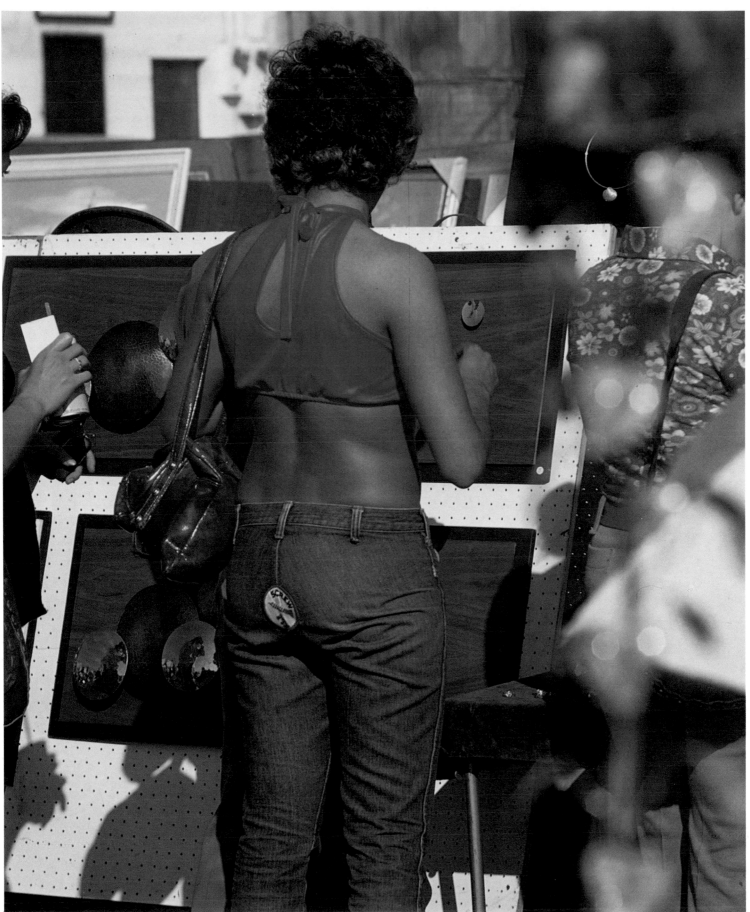

A DAY IN VENICE

Callisthenics and gluttony, beauty and despair, sea, sand and asphalt, style and fashion, drugs and drink, wheels and frisbees, oil rigs and palm trees, the Sunday voyeur's delight.... Sit outside the sidewalk café and feel the excesses lap over you!

Tee shirt girl

Buy a headset

Cheap skates

Roll on baby

Dangerous

I got rhythm

I got muscles

I got stoned

Easter bunny

Save a skate

Paddle tennis

Rest a little

Skate a little

No disguising nature

They all have

Save a soul

Heel

Solitary confinement

Verdigris

Reflections

The way to arrive

The Green Door

Too clean for Venice

Smog

Sea Edge

Playground

WEDDINGS AND FUNERALS

Strolling along the beautifully kept walks one listens to soft music broadcast from amplifiers concealed in rose bushes. It is at once an art gallery, a Gretna Green marriage mart and a place where the dead can be tucked away with as little sorrow as one can bury a tin can in the backyard.

Carey McWilliams

Welcome

What does Forest Lawn Say?

and bury Daddy too

and hope

Hispanic colour scheme

Tomb for Jeremy Dixon

Low Rider Wedding

Tomb for Ed Jones

8 months is urgent

I got roots

Take your choice

Welcome home

Even when you are dead you have to have a conscience

No comment

They seem to be getting the wrong food

Roast a speciality

Uh Uh

Senator, I presume?

A Patriot to the last

Lasting longer at Forest Lawn

Veteran

RAZMATAZ

If you want the ultimate in friendly gregarious good-humoured America, don't fail to see a USC 'homecoming' game. Kids aged from 7 to 70 eat, drink and emote in a mist of bucolic delight—champagne on the lawn, a Henry VIII picnic lunch, Scottish pipers, marching bands, belly dancers from the Moorea Trojans! ancient alumni and trim-hipped freshwomen ablaze in maroon and gold, a horse more famous than 'Trigger'. And if your battered eyeballs permit it, you can even see the football game.

A Moorea Trojan!

The Homecoming Game

Look, no hands

Belly laughs

The horse, The horse

Ecstasy reigns

The conquest continues

It's not the Black Watch

No, I am not Charlie White

Tommy Trojan

Push 'em back

A class of '29

Where's the food?

Here's the food!

We can't lose

We don't lose

200 yards later

Let go my hand and show him your red card

Class of '94

Rah Rah

No aggro

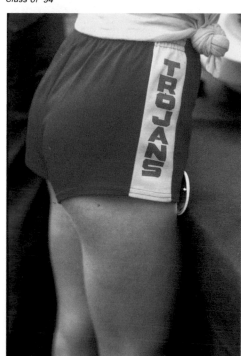
California thigh

California thighs

THE CAR CULT AND NAMEPLATES

The car cult exemplified by the New West Ferrari cover seems to have provided LA with more Rolls Royces than London, more Porsches than Frankfurt, more Ferraris than Rome. It also offers the eye a line in number plates that leaves one with a Cheshire cat expression on almost every journey.

 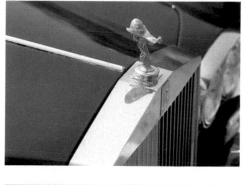

Fetish finish absorbs the Angeleno—trucker, collector or cop. It's all in the bodywork

WHEELS

A typical Angeleno rides to and from work, to and from shopping and to and from a Dodger game or a swap meet in a flat, soft, sealed, rolling jukebox along with his thoughts, rock music, sigalert bulletins, warnings of freeway congestion ... but everybody doesn't have a car!

Peter Plagens

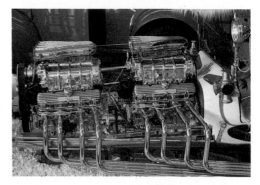

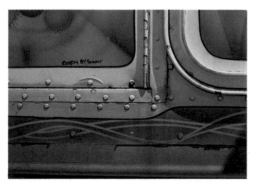

SIGNS

'Novelty catalogue drawing is not so bad if you look at it right. Cadillac Fins and Donut whitewalls are really pretty groovy, professional football is obscene, but some of the heaviest

people super-dig it, so why don't you? Sparkle front apartments all in a row make a nifty limited edition, a bullet through the eyeball in 70 mm colour, but it's OK if you are an ultra violence

'relevant' architecture. You do enough of these numbers and pretty soon your

dancing in your head ...'   Peter Plagens

jack will speak to you

BEVERLY HILLS LANDSCA

Like all irrigated civilisation, the land has a certain air of unreality about it ... all green things grow here with speed, continuity and abandon, so that a sense of permanency is gained but it is only a permanence that is skin deep ... there is a sense of having strayed into one of Mr Wells' 'Utopias'.

Maxwell Armfield, 1925, on LA

Scottish Baror

Breakfast in the Polo Lounge

Streets are n

Guess there is a house behind

Kitsch, Mo

Palms,

Palms, foliage and smog

New England, Beverly Hills

Painted genitals

Sunday papers

Manicurist art

Silver sprinklers

Sugar coated sculpture

Hacienda living

Landscape detail

Christmas allsorts

Wemple landscape

America the brave

Wilshire fountain

135

GINGERBREAD AND KITSCH

The reason for multiple images in this section is the need to underline Los Angeles as the city of excess. It isn't difficult to find a hundred or a thousand gingerbreads—this is no Jencksian voyage of discovery, it's a steal. The gingerbreads, kitsch, Victorian million dollar homes and crud stuccos occur in their legions down every suburban street, off-strip bolt hole or scrubby hillside in Los Angeles. Finding the sneaky Schindler or the camouflaged Neutra . . . that's the problem.

Hansel and Gretel House

Hansel and Gretel House, detail

Gingerbread Bungalow

The Witch's House

Gingerbread Court

Adapted tract

Gingerbread detail

Reverse colour scheme

Cake culture

Rustic revival

Welcome home

Your basic angel

Think thin

Mythology rampant

Morgue Modern

Don't trust anybody

Balanced entry

The Dog and Foliage Show

Waiting for Halloween

Angelic entry

Chateau entry

Sudden fancy

Bondage entry

137

Suburban housing in LA offers a variety of styling and parody. Chateaux interspersed with Castles interspersed with Forts interspersed with Pot Boiler Modern interspersed with Modern

interspersed with Hansel and Gretel, Ruretania and Transylvania—very often with the same floor plan.

Victorians, on the other hand, demonstrate individuality and an extraordinary craft-spirit. They are not as pretty as their San Francisco counterparts, but their vigour, detail and sense of

re-discovery make them collectors' items.

Charles Lagreco
POPULAR ARCHITECTURE IN LOS ANGELES

Your friendly Realtor

Watch Tower

Freeway at Dusk

DRIVING YOUR WAY THROUGH LOS ANGELES

As the transition ramp moves into the driver's line of vision, bunches of glaring red tail-lights warn of the problem ahead. The flow slows, then stops, and driver and car pause, suspended above the crossing streams of vehicles below on the San Diego and Santa Monica Freeway. The driver, momentarily free from the prerequisites of control, scans the Basin. On the right, the flatlands stretch toward punctuated distant hills, Baldwin, and still further to Palos Verdes, and the street grid dominates in an undistinguished landscape of isolated buildings. To the left and ahead, the driver can see through his windshield the unyielding march of Wilshire Corridor buildings swelling at Beverly Hills and Century City and ultimately at its downtown origins. The concentration of buildings in Hollywood, against the backdrop of the coastal range, provides another clear reference. Behind, the Santa Monica Bay stands framed by the natural topography of the Basin. 'Santa Anas' have provided what scale, lifestyle, and concentrated pollution have conspired to deny—a coherent image of L A.

Yet this is not surprising in a city where public space is largely organised and perceived through its relationship with the automobile. The driver could construct an introductory sampler of popular form: illustrating this sometimes symbiotic relationship, touching on every aspect of life in the metropolitan area, and spanning the currents and counter-currents of popular taste. For in fact, the idea of Los Angeles is unalterably dependent on the idea of the automobile and its much heralded independent mobility; mobility which provides access to the contrasts of widely divergent activities and environments ('*From the desert to the sea, from the mountains to the shore ...*,' Jerry Dumphy, KABC News); mobility; not preordained perhaps, yet spurred by the profusion of resources and opportunity, and hastened by conspiratorial corporate actions to eliminate the competition of the transit network, already full-blown when the car made its impact known.

POPULAR FORM AS SEEN FROM THE CAR

Chapter One: Gassing Up, Getting Ready to Roll
Roadside stand with cafe. Pump as equipment
Vernacular gas station garage.
Popular style imposed: Spanish Revival; Theme stations—Richfield Tower; Art Deco; Modern; International Style
Prefabrication: Functional tin can; Suburban integration; Ranch Style; French

Chapter Two: On the Street Where You Live ...
Single-family: Van Nuys—typical anywhere, north-south residential streets on the flats. *Beverly Hills*—typical flats, million dollar residential street, wealthy ghetto. *Watts*—typical flats, residential street in economically deprived area. *Rolling Hills*—security community with alternate lifestyle, ie horses. *Manhattan Beach*—water view with parking problems. *Santa Monica Canyon*—asserting the 'natural' landscape. *Mount Olympus*—ecological disaster and bad taste all-in-one. *Old Pasadena*—the legacy of planned landscape. *Westlake Village*—self-consciously suburban with all the right market features. *Malibu*—the ultimate sacrifice, fulfilled fantasy.

Multi-family: *West Hollywood*—apartment block with facade gesture for identity, very dense. *Brentwood*—newer version of high-density apartment living, Barrington, north of Wilshire. *Wilshire, West LA*—high-rise condo and apartment slabs. *Park La Brea*—shades of New York public housing in cross-point high-rise. *Casa de Vita*—Mega apartment project with 'walk-up' scale community-concept-theme. *Public housing*—East Los Angeles Project. *Retirement apartment*—6th Street across from MacArthur Park. *Prefab retirement*—Little Tokyo Demonstration Project. *Hollywood court. Main Street*—flop houses, converted old hotels, missions, skid row.

Chapter Three: On the Way to ... Drive-In
Restaurants: *Fast Food*—McDonald's, Jack-in-the-Box, Taco Bell, Tommy's, Rampart at Beverly. *Car Hop*—Dolores' in Beverly Hills on Wilshire; Tiny Naylor's Sunset at La Brea. *Family*—Bob's Big Boy, Foothill Boulevard. *Coffee Shop*—24 Hours: Denney's, Googies. *Freeway Restaurants*—West Covina at the San Bernardino Freeway. *Restaurant Row*—La Cienega. *Ethnic*—Chinatown, Broadway north; Little Tokyo, 1st Street; Korean, Olympic; Olivera Street, Mexican. *Theme*—New England fishing village, Ports of Call, San Pedro.
Services: *Bank, Cleaner, Groceries, Car Wash, and Dairy,* are all to be found on any strip or commercial street in Los Angeles. *Office*—6th and Coronado (park at your desk).

Chapter Four: Going Shopping
7–11 Market, corner grocery LA style. *Convenience shopping. The Supermarket. Retail Centres*—ethnic centres, eg Chinatown; speciality, eg garment district; associations, eg Miracle Mile. *Regional Centres*—Del Amo; Fox Hills. *Unique Experiences*—Farmers' Market; Central Market; Flea Market, Rose Bowl; Vendors, Venice Ocean Front; Westwood Village; Rodeo Drive, The Golden Triangle.

Chapter Five: Cruising—LA's Answer to the Promenade
Hollywood Boulevard—theatres, people, etc.
Sunset Boulevard—billboards, view of city edge.
Whittier Boulevard—East Los Angeles low-riders.
Van Nuys Boulevard—Valley custom cars, nite.
The Endless Strip—Ventura Boulevard.
The Coast Highway—Route 1, the Palisades.
Mulholland Drive—from the Hollywood to the San Diego.

Chapter Six: Aberrations—Primarily Pedestrian
Ocean Front Walk, Venice Beach
Broadway, Med. promenade Chicago style
Santa Monica Palisade Park, Ocean Boulevard
Westwood Village, Westwood Boulevard

Chapter Seven: View From the Fast Lane—the 65 mph Perspective (55 for the Record)
Foothill Freeway, view through Valley to downtown and beyond, at the edge looking down.
Santa Monica Freeway, night view from the flats to the hills, paralleling the Wilshire Corridor.
Through the Pass: Hollywood Freeway—Cahuenga Pass; San Diego—Sepulveda Pass; San Bernardino—Kellog Hill.

ETHNIC

Be it ever so ethnic there's no place like home!

From the open air prison of Watts to the Chatteaux of Bel Air, Los Angeles offers to the inquisitive punter all the options—Korean village or Chinese stage set, Japanese raw fish to real Kosher meatballs; Hispanic 'Matrimonios Urgentes' to the dismal parodies of Irish bars. Los Angeles is not just the truest conceivable representation of the whole American face, urban, big town, little town, as described by Garrett. In recent times it has started to represent the face of a wayward world.

DRIVE-IN CULTURE

Legless Angelenos are blessed with compensations. You can drive into practically everything, fill her up, eat your way through a trough of junk, take a room for the night, cash a cheque,

wash the tin jukebox you're driving ready to take a spin on the old meatgrinder, known as the LA Freeway System, to meet many more of the similarly afflicted. And if Cal Tran monitors

you correctly your jaunt will be at a smooth 55 mph and you may even score! God Bless America, you treat me so well!

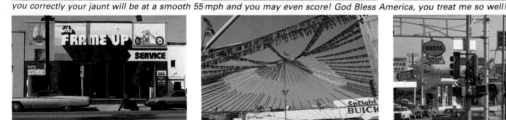

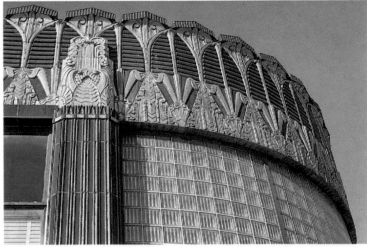

If your bag is detail, Los Angeles offers more camera frames than street signs, from a bank, to the Paradise Ballroom, Tiffany glass, Coca Cola ad, street signing, trash cans, and religious

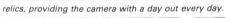

relics, providing the camera with a day out every day.

143

Rancho Santa Anita

Children's Dentist

Rampant apartments

RIP

Your regular Crocker Bank

Down Town

'Moderne' Court

Wrong side of the tracks

Can you believe LA?

Decorating Watts

1930s Building, Huntingdon Drive

Beach housing

Pasadena solid

Peeling, 1930s

1930s corner detail

2442 Eagle Rock

Mormon Temple

Richfield Oil

Echo Park

Reflections Santa Monica

Mall

Griffith Park from Hollywood

La Brea

Quiet freeway

Tract, Beverly Glen

Palm House

Gamblers residence

Chateauville

Fairfax

Beverly Canyon

Belair

Alvarado

Fairfax Area

Beverly Hills

Santa Monica

Richfield Building

A DRIVE ALONG SUNSET BOULEVARD

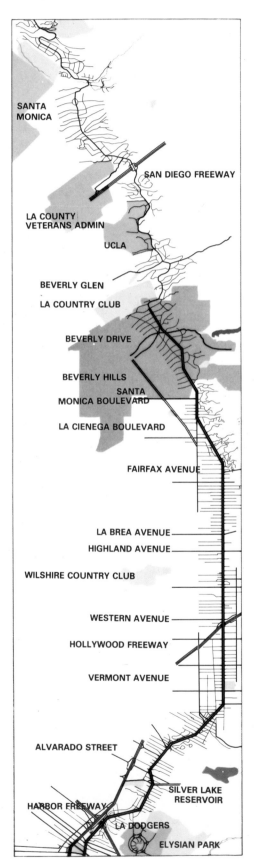

A homage to the street—long streets, fat streets, thin streets, flat streets, hilly streets. Mount Olympus, Hawthorne, Beverly and Wilshire provide a weird assemblage of frantic strip graffiti or a paeon to the palm tree culture. In the end it's a toss up—a regular cruise down Sunset taking in the latest billboards, or a leafy crawl through Beverly Glen, finishing on the Mulholland Switchback. (Incidentally, if you are anxious to look for the longest street in Los Angeles, try Sepulveda Boulevard, it's 30.8 miles long.) In order to demonstrate the variety, the next four pages are devoted to a Sunday drive along the length of Sunset Boulevard, followed by a drive along the length of Wilshire. Both sequences demonstrate the external variety in both a commercial and aesthetic sense. These few photographs are only a very small sampling, but they do give an indication that a drive down the main drags is mandatory. Go slowly, slowly, not just for the parallel happenings but also for the sneaky views at cross junctions.

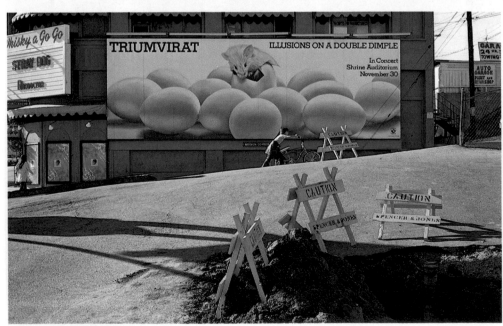

A DRIVE ALONG WILSHIRE BOULEVARD

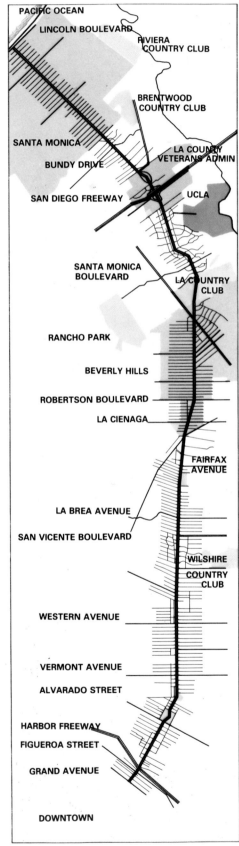

Ron Herron and Derek Walker
TOURIST LOS ANGELES

Despite the 50 thousand members of the British colony in Los Angeles, the humorous documentation of Art Seidenbaum and Jack Smith, the hip sixties mythology padlocked to the persons of Reyner Banham and Tom Wolfe, the straight ace prose of Carey McWilliams, and the suicidal, smog-bound rhetoric of Peter Plagens, we reckon this particular section is our baby. As regular tourists and occasional teachers, we subscribe to the band of brothers who agree with Ray Bradbury's 'noxious futuromystical treacle' that Los Angeles is the Best Place in America (Esquire, October 1972).

We don't quite hit it with the style attributed to our predecessors at the turn of the century. 'The party of English gentlemen who left Santa Barbara a few days ago' wrote a local reporter, 'are reported to be riding around Los Angeles with seventeen valises, six pocket flasks, 21 demijohns, three repeating rifles, twelve mosquito nets, five alpaca dusters, four Ulsters, ten trunks, three plug hats, six lunch baskets, eight umbrellas, five canes, six pairs of blankets, twelve pairs of rubber boots, but no other baggage worth mentioning.' We do, however, hit it regularly, become more fascinated with each visit, and even if we don't make the Beverly Hills Hotel every time, we come away with sufficient sunshine, juice and adrenalin to last through another British winter.

Tourism is not new to Los Angeles—it's a long established tradition. Carey McWilliams vividly described a typical tour arranged 80 years ago:

A miniature grand tour was organised for winter tourists in Southern California. With scarcely a single exception the winter tourists made a trip to Venice; ascended Mount Lowe and stayed overnight in the Alpine Inn; visited the Mission at San Gabriel (where they bought as souvenirs Mission, poppy and poinsettia pillows); crossed the channel to Catalina Island and took a ride on the famous 'glass-bottom boats'; visited the Cawston Ostrich Farm in South Pasadena and Busch's Gardens in Pasadena; lunched at the Mission Inn in Riverside; spent a day at Lucky Baldwin's Santa Anita ranch; visited Paul de Longpre's garden home in Hollywood to purchase one of his flower paintings; and attended a 'Bird Recital' by the California School of Artistic Whistling at Blanchard Hall (decorated with palm trees and bird cages, Blanchard Hall was one of the prize exhibits of the period). A procession of tourists attended the weekly 'complimentary musicale' sponsored by a local furniture company, where a young lady sang songs in 'four different languages' and every visitor was presented with a picture postcard of Los Angeles as it looked in 1880. As minor attractions there were the alligator farm, the lion farm and the endless winter revival meetings.

From 1900 to 1920 Los Angeles was essentially a tourist town. Like most tourist towns, it had its share of freaks, sideshows, novelties and showplaces. Ducks waddled along the streets with advertisements painted on their backs; six foot nine pituitary giants with sa[...] signs stalked the downtown streets; while t[...] people carrying Bibles in their hands and sin[...] marched in evangelical parades. With its [...] shooting galleries, curio shops, health lect[...] night movies, Main Street became a honk[...] that never closed. During the winter r[...] Angeles was, in fact, a great circus without[...]
The circus continues unabated, and the [...]

complexity of rib-tickling sideshows, predominantly based on the show business ethic. Seidenbaum would caution you that the best way to survive in Los Angeles is to have an amusing act, and to put the best possible face on that act... You never know when you will find your next booking, and everybody but everybody auditions daily in Los Angeles.

The maître D at the Sidewalk Cafe, Venice, is black, handsome, immaculate in a vicuna suit, silk shirt and tie. He also happens to be on roller skates. Outside the railings the tee shirt lady, elegant and well-stacked, bends to sell a 'Safety Shirt' to an overweight victim of the roller skate mania—he and his broken leg are borne away by an evangelical group of asphalt life guards keeping time with the rock standards emerging from a tattooed dwarf selling earphone radios. The paramedics trail obligingly after a geriatric group of joggers on San Vicente. A flush of blue-rinsed, blue-minked ladies picket Sunset Boulevard on Sunday afternoon with placards marked KAHOS—exhorting a reluctant world to Keep All Hookers Off Sunset.

Across the road Tower Records, low on decor, high on value, throbs with quadrophonic sound and mating calls in a dozen languages, as locust-like Europeans scavenge the warehouse shelves for cut-price discs and tapes. Swedes, Italians, English and French stagger out with a year's supply like happy junkies with freshly laundered withdrawal symptoms.

Westwood Village on Saturday evening provides entertainment in every doorway. Blacked-up Scott Joplins, fire-eaters, jugglers, illusionists, evangelists, nymphets, roller dancers and bondage freaks jostle for position and the inevitable collection. At the same time, Van Nuys and Broadway provide a cavalcade of low riders. The dresses are rampant bougainvillaea in mode with overtones of Carmen Jones. You may even get a wedding party with twelve Bo-Peep bridesmaids and a befuddled father slightly embarrassed to be so close to the ground while driving.

'For the homeless', comments William Ellis, 'Los Angeles is a favoured city. One seldom needs a heated grate for sleeping, or the Army greatcoat, longtime skid-row fashion in colder climate. The derelict in Los Angeles appears to be a healthier specimen than his brethren elsewhere. One is struck, too, by the number of women who work the trash baskets and doze in the musty hallways'. Ellis goes on to describe one woman, between 35 and 40, whom he saw every day for almost a month, and she always wore the same clothes. Her shoes were pink ballerina slippers and it was easy to see they were too small because her toes were bunched up in knots the size of lemons. Her blue nylon jacket was too big and so were the dungerees and the faded, torn blouse. One day when she stopped him to ask for a cigarette, he noticed her hands. They were pale and smooth—the hands of a contessa—and the long, slender fingers tapered off to flawlessly polished nails. Those hands graced that haggard body as the eyelashes of a giraffe grace that silly face. 'You have beautiful hands' he [...]eal herself as the daughter of a [...] some abolished monarchy in [...]l you see, honey, I don't do a lot [...]area of Beverly Hills looking for [...]ds isn't a crime, but it can be [...] intent, and I can recommend a [...]Hills Highway Patrol, who inevit-[...] of jaunt. Apart from a natural

mental blockage concerning the use of the human leg, they respond badly to enquiries on the folklore of the neighbourhood. One place to walk but not to enter is Rodeo Drive, which makes the rue St Honoré look like Petticoat Lane pricewise. The sights are pure LA: pampered, miniature, decorated dogs, straight from the beautician; Ted Lapidus and Hermes chic; and a trail of long legged golden beauties poised for investment ... not for tourists. But if you really want to invest an hour in the ultimate consumer society, check out the Rich Boys Toy Shop on Santa Monica.

One mandatory indulgence is breakfast in the Polo Lounge, Beverly Hills Hotel. It's a case of eggs on ego as the telephones are passed from table to table, minor celebrities are pointlessly paged, and stone-faced producers listen impassively to the mounting hysteria of a hopeful hustler.

The city really is a voyeur's delight: the evening view from Griffith Park Observatory, the sunset over Santa Monica and Malibu, the Japanese toyshop downtown, a USC/UCLA track meet, a glimpse of children stealing grapes in Central Market, a browse round Hennessy & Engels, lunch at Lawry's Garden Centre on San Antonio, dinner at Moon Shadows or Holiday House at Malibu, Echo Park, Venice on Sunday, the horses at Santa Anita, the Dogers and the Reds at Chavez Ravine, Emmet Wemple's landscape trip—seashore, hillside, mountain desert and back in one day, Forest Lawn and the Animal Cemeteries, Hollywood and Vine, and so to bed at the Madonna Inn!

Inevitably one has become preoccupied with the free circus of LA. We have almost forgotten the commercial products—Disneyland, Magic Mountain, Marine World, Marina del Rey, the Ports of Call, Knottsberry Farm, Universal Studios, the Queen Mary, the Stars' Houses, Hearst Castle at San Simeon, Huntington Park, Foxhill Mall, the Galleries of LA and Pasadena, but there's always a next time! Drive carefully and remember Ronald Weier's cryptic warning in Licensed to Kill (1968):

The American motorist thinks of driving as an evil sort of manual labour which is beneath his dignity. Shifting gears is only for poor people and hot rodders. The affluent simply don't want to engage in the tedious and difficult task of physically driving an automobile. Most are content just to sit back and relax in their thickly padded seats and drown themselves in the luxury of having nothing to do behind the wheel except curse occasionally at the people who pass them on the right while they're busy daydreaming in the passing lane. The average motorist, with countless mechanical servants to perform his job for him, has very few mechanical responsibilities behind the wheel. Because he has nothing to do, he also has little to think about, and as a result he can actually go into a semi-trance while he is at the wheel. He has so many gadgets to help him drive that he often delegates to his mechanical servants more driving responsibility than they can possibly handle.

Have a happy day!

Angels Flight. Early tourist trap sadly lost to Downtown

Rosebowl Pasadena

Marineland

Rides

Santa Monica playground

Queen Mary, Long Beach

Ocean University

Magic Mountain

Marineland

Ports O' Call

Ports O' Call

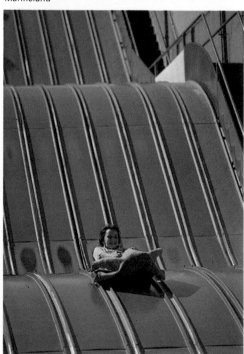
Slide Santa Monica

Long Beach

Knottsberry Farm

MOVIE THEATRES

The Alex Cinema

Graumann's Chinese Theatre

The Arlington Cinema

1930 Premiere Chinese Theatre

The Climax Theatre, La Cienega

Freemont Cinema

Neon detail

Cinema Hoarding

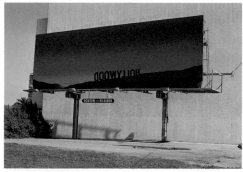
Hollywood Billboard

Arlington at night

Bert Stern's Marylyn Monroe

'After 1920 a new heterogenous tide of migrants brought still further cultural changes to Los Angeles. The motion picture industry attracted odd and freekish types: dwarfs, pygmies, one-eyed sailors, show people, misfits and 50,000 wonder-struck girls. The easy ways of Hollywood drew pimps, gamblers, racketeers and confidence men ... times don't change but many of the splendid movie houses, a testament to the period, wither and die.'
                              Carey McWilliams on Hollywood

Stars' footprints at the Chinese Theatre

Hollywood Boulevard

155

DAY TO DAY

Main Street, Disneyland

Riverboat, Disneyland

McArthur Park Parade

Night, Disneyland

Fairy Castle, Disneyland

Beach, Santa Monica

Night, Disneyland

Marina

Electrical Parade

Disneyland

Beach scene

No alcohol

Balloons, Disneyland

Birds along the shore

Beach scene

Shopping Centre entertainment

Junk food

Kite flying, Griffith Park

Shoe store, Santa Monica

Sunday market

Fish

Pepsi Parlour

Los Angeles sunset

Foxhills Mall

Ted Lapidus Rodeo

Griffiths Park Observatory

Central market

Farmer's Market

157

Hearst Castle, San Simeon

Hearst Castle, San Simeon

The Madonna Inn

Hearst Castle, San Simeon

Hearst Castle, San Simeon

The Madonna Inn

Hearst Castle, San Simeon

Hearst Castle, San Simeon

The Madonna Inn

The Madonna Inn

Hearst Castle, San Simeon

Hearst Castle, San Simeon

The Madonna Inn

Goodyear Blimp

Lotus

Thousand Oaks

Universal Studios

Exit to Chinatown

Huntingdon Gardens

Parting of the Red Sea

Jaws

Huntingdon Gardens

Huntingdon Gardens

Huntingdon Gardens

Huntingdon Gardens

Huntingdon Gardens

One of the best loved of LA Monuments, the Astounding Watts Towers by Simon Rodia is an incredible testament to an astonishing man.

160

David Brindle
THE APPROPRIATE FINISH

Edward Ruscha, City, 1969

Producing a fine finish is one of the things Los Angeles does extremely well. From the machining and assembling of spacecraft in dust-free plastic tents, through the meticulous manicuring of the landscape, to the drilled executing of the Ram's offensive line, a thing well finished is enjoyed as a special quality of life. This is not to say that these precision aspects of the LA environment are uptight, hard-edged or lacking in spontaneity, as this is not the case.

The art included here all has, to the Angeleno, the joy of the graceful concrete toughness of a freeway interchange or the yellow blend to green blend to blue of a Curt Brubaker custom car. Eric Orr, for instance, is appropriately elegant with either the fragility of finely ground edged glass with pale metallic particles changing hue, or the lead and gold 'Chemical Light' bas-reliefs which he has recently produced, where the edges distinctly say lead. The term 'Fetish-Finish' has been used to describe some LA artists for over a decade now. The phrase, while having a great journalistic ring, is off base as it implies self-consciousness and over-inflated technique. The artist's craftsmanship and his enjoyment of it seem inevitable and a proper outcome of LA.

The areas of art included are further linked in that, while not unique to Los Angeles, it is to that city that they owe their reputation. Those who have not yet been welcomed to LA build their expectations on the Big Art of the billboards, the aerospace glossies and technical drawings; and the Big Orange does better with the Fine Art of environment and performance than the Big Apple on the other coast.

Big Art

Bumper-to-bumper manoeuvring along the Sunset Strip, particularly at night, is cruising a colossal art gallery. There are regulars who drive the Strip once a month to see the latest 60 × 18 foot Show Biz promotions, lit more brilliantly than any living colour. Big Art began in the Thirties selling Del Monte canned fruit, Ford autos and Coke in what were then fields, along the roads taking the weekenders to the ocean. Legend has it that the Strip became synonymous with Big Art in 1953, when a Las Vegas casino paraded bathing-suited girls around a swimming pool from midday to midnight, with a promotional billboard behind them. Immediately an aspiring actress, envying the attention given to the Casino, had a board painted to publicise herself. No one remembers who she was.

The Strip is not the only prime Big Art location. Along the freeways and particularly Century Boulevard leading to the International Airport are 'Fly TWA', 'Drive Chevy', 'Drink Coke', 'Burn Gas' and those which cause the accidents 'Beautiful tan, Beautiful skin. Coppertone'. While the cost of Big Art is inexpensive, $18000 to $3500 for a prime location, including the painting, the billboard is a big dollar industry. More than $3 million a year is paid to the owners of the land on which the boards stand, and over half a million is spent on lighting.

The process of the hand-painted boards starts with the precision scaled photography of art work on 8 × 10 inch Kodalith ortho film with an Estar base. Using two projectors, one for each half, a positive image is shone on to a 50 × 22 foot high wall of grounded fine copper wire mesh covered with white paper. An electric pencil tracing the lines of the artwork causes an arc to the copper, burning tiny holes through the paper. The perforated paper is taken to the painting studio and hung against the prepared plywood billboards. Bags of porous cloth filled with ground charcoal are beaten against the paper, forcing the charcoal through the holes onto the boards, leaving an accurate enlargement of the original artwork. The artists use weather-resistant oil-based paints, applied by brush to colour out the artwork. A simple board of lettering may take as little as half a day, while the complex work with many figures may take as long as a month. In both cases the price of the board would be the same. If the art is to be kept alive it is repainted every four months. A set of boards will be retired after about 18 months, by which time it may have had 14 displays. Big Art is very short-lived.

Leonard Rubinstein, in Graphis 199, explains how Big Art is a part of the traditional American Art:

Since colonial times photographic realism has been an American Tradition in art: Charles Willson Peale, Gilbert Stuart portraits, William Harnett's fool-the-eye paintings, landscapes by the Hudson River School, the work of Winslow Homer, Frederick Remington and Charles Russet's illustrations of the Old West, the Wyeths—grandfather, father and son, Reginald Marsh, Norman Rockwell and a host of others. Big Art is a titanic, dramatic continuation of this native American style.

The industry is currently previewing pneumatic Big Art. Shown protruding from the boards is the hand of a giant which crushes a beer can, by extracting and re-inflating the beer can. The sales banter beckons: *'Here, at last, is a new dimension in outdoor advertising, a medium that meets the requirements of the Space Age. Using this medium; your message will literally leap out of the board and demand the attention of anyone who passes it'.* That should keep us in our Chevys.

Image Art

Angelenos, like natives of many places, seem to be too close to identify the uniqueness of their place. Two master interpreters, Edward Ruscha and David Hockney, are from places both miles and spirits apart from LA. Ruscha was brought up in Oklahoma City, Nebraska, and Hockney in Bradford, Yorkshire.

Ruscha and Hockney make those images which, once seen, lodge in the mind as a perfect dream, and LA becomes them. While Ruscha has previously painted Big Art, a Hollywood backwards, Hockney is presently painting a 20 × 9 foot 'Santa Monica Boulevard', and a piece of proper Big art which is a billboard to go over a restaurant, which will show the restaurant from the same viewpoint. (And the billboard?).

Big Industry Art

Since the mid-1930s, Los Angeles has been the centre of the American aircraft industry; and, since 1948, with the first missile production and firing, Los Angeles has also been the centre of the space programme. When the industry developed rapidly, there was a severe shortage of trained personnel for the gamut of job skills. An organisation called TIMA (Technical Illustrators Management Association) was formed and was successful in encouraging trade schools to provide courses in the illustrative skills. After being very influential it declined as the aerospace industry was cut back in the late 1960s, leaving behind the education in the colleges.

There are four types of drawing in aerospace: industrial illustration, technical illustration, production drawing and automated drawing. Industrial illustration is simulation painting, as true-to-life as possible, intended to show the form of a vehicle prior to being modelled, or to portray a situation expected in the future, like a launching. The artist is frequently the form-maker for the systems-design engineers. Working closely with the engineers, they will sketch suggestions of how the vehicle will shape out, or how the event will occur. The life of the illustration is over once a photograph of a mock-up or the actual hardware is built. It is amazing to compare the accuracy of the pre-event illustrations with the photographs of the actual event. The painting, usually on mylar or card about 30 × 20 inches, are in gouache or artists colours, and occasionally in crayon. An illustration will average one week from beginning the cartoon to completion.

Technical illustration is black and white explanatory drawings of hardware, showing its manufacture, servicing or safety procedures, usually to be used in manuals. These drawings are Rapidograph ink-line on polyester film (which is as inert as mylar, yet less costly and less damaging to the pens.) Architects take heart, for careful examination shows that aerospace drafters also have problems joining curved and straight lines.

Production drawings are in pencil or ink on polyester, and usually drawn, as are technical illustrations, in dimetric projection. As aeroplanes and space vehicles are not easily explained by plans and elevations, the industry has developed this three-dimensional drawing system which is a refinement of the 30°-30° isometric projection. The differences are that the angles of the side planes are 15°-by-15° and that two scales are used, one for the height plan of 0·963433 of the actual height, as used on isometric, and the other of 0·732051 for the depth or horizontal plane. The advantages of such a system are that it gives a realistic view with little distortion, is easier to draw than perspective, and the standardisation of format allows drawings to be used for engineering, manufacture, repair and parts manuals. Trimetric projection is also used. Whereas a dimetric projection of a cube will have two equal faces, the trimetric will have three different faces and scales.

Automated drawings have an increasing scope by taking over repetitive drawing and producing complex systems studies with scale changes, multiple viewpoints and flow sequences. Automated systems have clear advantages in time and cost saving. Rockwell International's B-1 Division uses a computer-based automatic drafting system which produces drawings in half the time, at a 30% cost saving. In this class careful examination of the drawings shows that the machine can effect perfect curve to straight-line sequences. However, the line looks incredibly nervous.

EDWARD RUSCHA

Edward Ruscha, Hollywood

Edward Ruscha, Swimming Pool Series

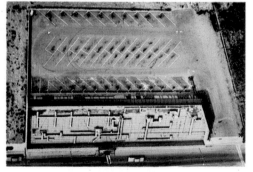

Edward Ruscha, Parking Series

DAVID HOCKNEY

David Hockney, Study for Santa Monica Boulevard, 1979

David Hockney, Divine, 1979

Hockney in LA

CHRIS BURDEN

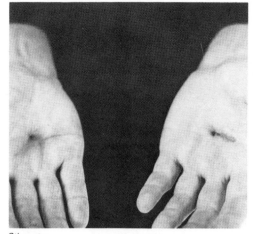

Stigmata

The Message

Merry Christmas from Chris Burden

Fine Art

When I visited Michael Brewster's studio I was left in a bare, converted shop, with a high ceiling and everything painted white. At one end was a step down to the old glass storefront with indoor palms and a view through louvers, across the Boardwalk, to the sand and sea. Then a deep vibrating sound, and I noticed the single speaker at the back of the room. As I walked to the speaker the sound increased and decreased, and I found spots of little or no sound and spots of considerable sound. It was like being in a thick invisible cloud. Acoustically the show is a wavelength phenomenon known as a 'standing wave', produced by a pure tone in a specific space. The sound wave resonates from the walls and focuses in various densities in particular areas, and exists as volumes and hollows in space. Brewster described the effect as sculpture to be seen by the Mind's Eye.

A demonstration of another piece was also in the empty room. This time a multiple 'clicking' from everywhere. There was no evidence of the sound's source. Embedded into the studio walls are mechanical devices by Brewster, beautifully made and hidden, all emitting regular clicks of the same tone. The timing devices are set to the same ten-second interval but the mechanism is not exact, and a growing deviation occurs between all the units, at first growing apart and then together, until the clicks become seemingly random. As I concentrated on the clickings they began to link across the room and along the walls in a changing pattern. Brewster explained that these were 'drawings', and that he enjoyed the uncontrolled random-ness of the clicks and was not interested in predicting patterns. Similar to the sound drawings are 'blinks', or light drawings. Precision-made small white lights floating in the studio sink, blinking in random patterns, were a mock-up for an ambitious event to be held in Venice, Italy.

A short walk south along the Venice Boardwalk past the reclining dogs and residents to another studio. This one was like Brewster's, a converted shop painted white, but it had work on the walls and in the space, and a simple table in the middle. This is Eric Orr's home and studio. In 1974 I had visited Cirrus Gallery for an exhibit by Orr called Zero Mass. It consisted of making an appointment to see two large spaces. The first space, in softened daylight, contained a large neat square of wind-blown sand like a rippled lake, and to one side a raised tatami mat platform with formal Japanese tea making utensils. Two or three people were in the space at a time and were served tea formally by a kimonoed Japanese woman while contemplating the waves of sand. The second space was large, of continous white paper with no light whatsoever. It took about 15 minutes before a faint, gentle glow gave me enough confidence and excitement to enter the space fully. It was completely disorientating; the walls and floor seemed not to exist; other visitors loomed up and then vanished as in a pale glowing fog. A very sensual experience.

The next Eric Orr exhibition I saw was also at Cirrus. It was a series of drawings on glass. They were planar perspectives of rooms drawn with subtle grades of gold, green, blue and purple, the spectrum quality of colour changing as viewed from varying angles. This process, developed with Larry Bell, is electromagnetic. A filament is heated in a vacuum chamber to a vapour state when the particles are transmitted and fused to the glass. The wavelength of the projection governs the spectrum colour and masking permits the 'drawing'. Many layers of varying colour are fused on top of each other. The finished glass is subtle, extremely rich and of the highest craftsmanship.

Orr's Studio had two such pieces displayed along with some simple square, gold panels, and an environment currently being worked on. This is a silent gold void of a particularly beautiful light. Orr says he wants to make the best space you've ever been in.

Another block down the Boardwalk past more palms, sand, bikes, skaters and more reclining dogs to Chris Burden's converted shop studio. Again the ubiquitous door gives the passer-by no clue as to how different and special is the space that is on the other side. There were dimes with wooden match sticks for guns, representing tanks, lined up over the floor in military discipline. Chris Burden gives performances. The events vary in scope and social comment. They may involve a seated audience or an unsuspecting passer-by. The success of the event is judged on the reactions of the people to a situation which is beyond their normal scope. Burden has other traits than the quality of finish or 'performance' which are also synonymous with LA. His work is extreme, physical and to the point. When his works involve extreme physical and mental conditioning, as many do, Burden is probably most interested in the preparation for the event and his control during the event. He sees his body and mind as items to be trained for special duty, somewhat like a Samurai or spaceman. His performances are simple and direct, as was 'Back to You':

Dressed only in pants, I was lying on a table inside a freight elevator ... next to me on the table was a small dish of 5/8″ steel push pins ... a sign in the elevator read, 'Please push pins into my body'. The volunteer stuck 4 pins into my stomach and 1 pin into my foot during the elevator trip ...

Similarly, while teaching at Simon Frazer University in Vancouver he was disappointed with the students resisting his coaxing to dig a ditch: *'Finally, I dug the ditch myself ... It wasn't an earthwork.'*

David Brindle

Chris Burden, Death Valley Ride

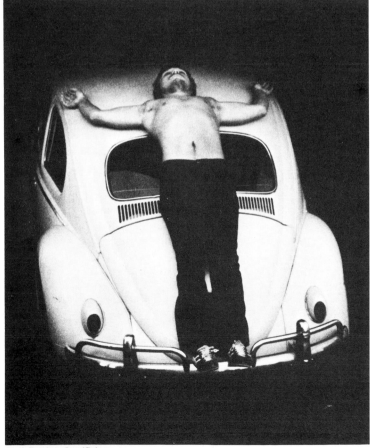

Chris Burden, Crucifixion

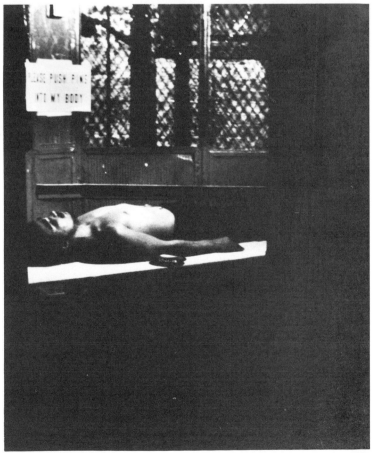

Chris Burden, Pin Cushion

165

FOSTER AND KLEISER

MARIO RUEDA

Johnny Mathis

Mario Rueda Master Printer

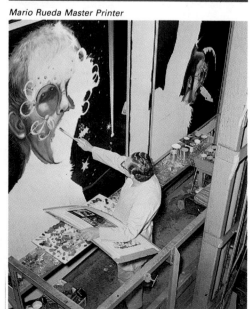

Elton John

ERIC ORR AND MICHAEL BREWSTER

Glass Drawing, 1978, Eric Orr

Acoustic Sculpture, 1976, Michael Brewster

A Slow Walking Wave, 1976, Michael Brewster

LARRY BELL AND ERIC ORR

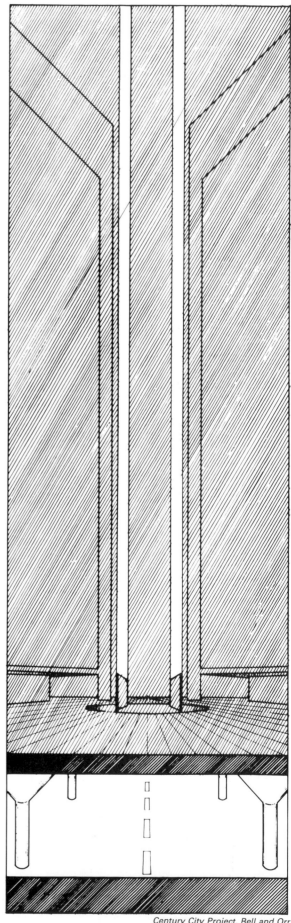

Century City Project, Bell and Orr

LARRY BELL, ERIC ORR AND MICHAEL BREWSTER

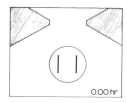

Two panels 396″ × 9″ × 162″ are positioned at the quarter points across the diameter of the grass circle, on axis with the triangular towers and the plaza in Century City.

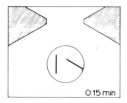

Each wall is finished in gold, and constructed hollow with an internal laser system. The system consists of a laser, a beam guide, and an array of beam reflectors. The beam guide sweeps the mirrored surfaces at a rate greater than the persistence of vision. The result is two sheets of blue laser light, planar extensions of the panels vertically to the cloud cover above. The system is composed entirely of existing technology. Wind or solar energy can be incorporated in generating the electricity needed to run the laser units.

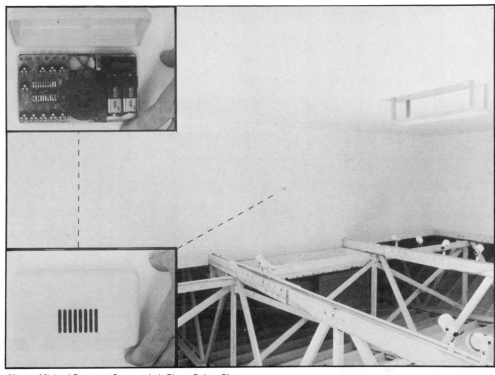

Above: Michael Brewster, Surrounded: Sharp Points Ringing, installation view, Cirrus Gallery, Los Angeles, May/June 1979. Upper right: detail, exterior of The Multi, a 4-channel adjustable sound source, 5½″ × 3½″ × 1¼″. Lower right: detail, interior of The Multi, showing batteries, high frequency loudspeaker and control board set for Surrounded: Sharp Points Ringing.
Right: Michael Brewster, Four Floating Flashers (one in Cutaway). Each measures 3½″ in height.
Below: Michael Brewster, Concentrate/Break-up. An exterior acoustic sculpture, Taraval Street pedestrian tunnel, San Francisco, California. Produced by CARP, January 1977. (p: Charles Christopher Hill).

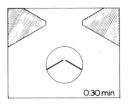

The walls have a pivoting time function, with respect to their positions relative to one another throughout the course of an hour's time. These movements repeat every hour.

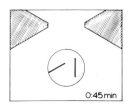

Through the course of 24 hours, the laser system would switch on before dusk and switch off after early morning. The effect is a gradual presence with the ON/OFF function being imperceptible.

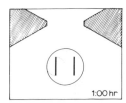

Century City Project, Bell and Orr

BIG ART

WALL PAINTINGS OF LOS ANGELES

FAS

Estrada Courts

Hoardings

Wall Mural

Children's Mural

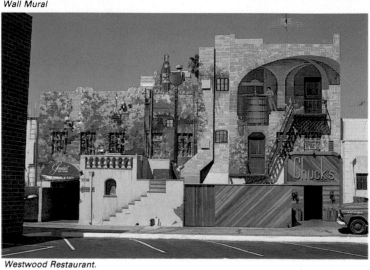

Westwood Restaurant.

Record Warehouse

Painting Hollister Street

1263 West Temple

Hart Street, Santa Monica

ART AND THE AEROSPACE INDUSTRY

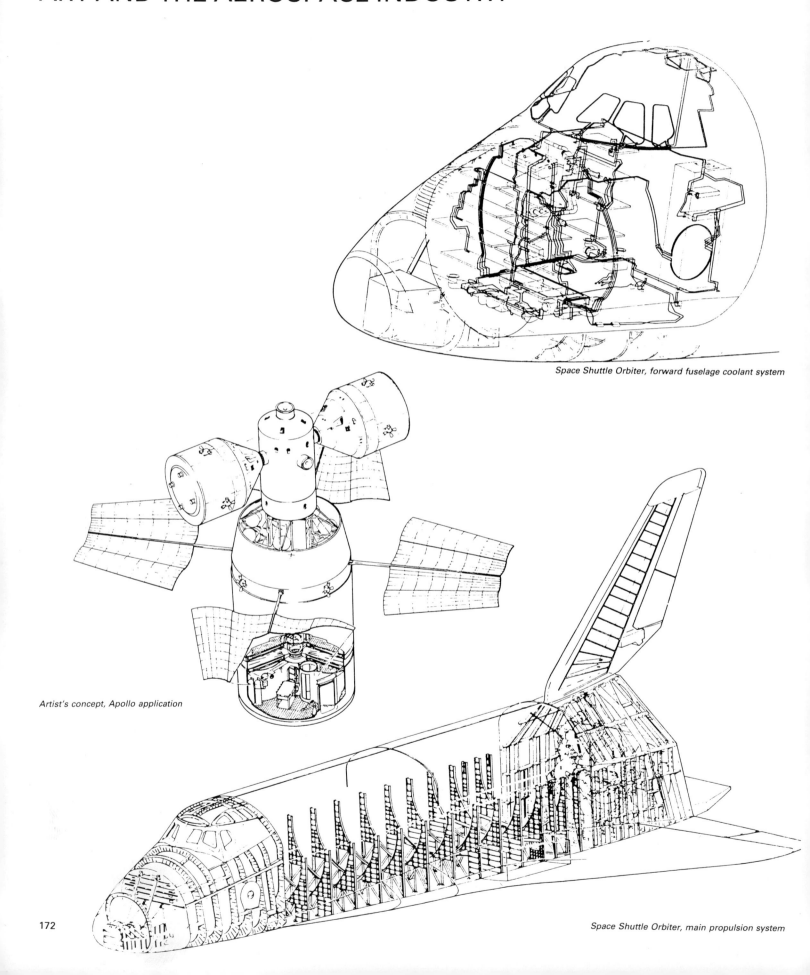

Space Shuttle Orbiter, forward fuselage coolant system

Artist's concept, Apollo application

Space Shuttle Orbiter, main propulsion system

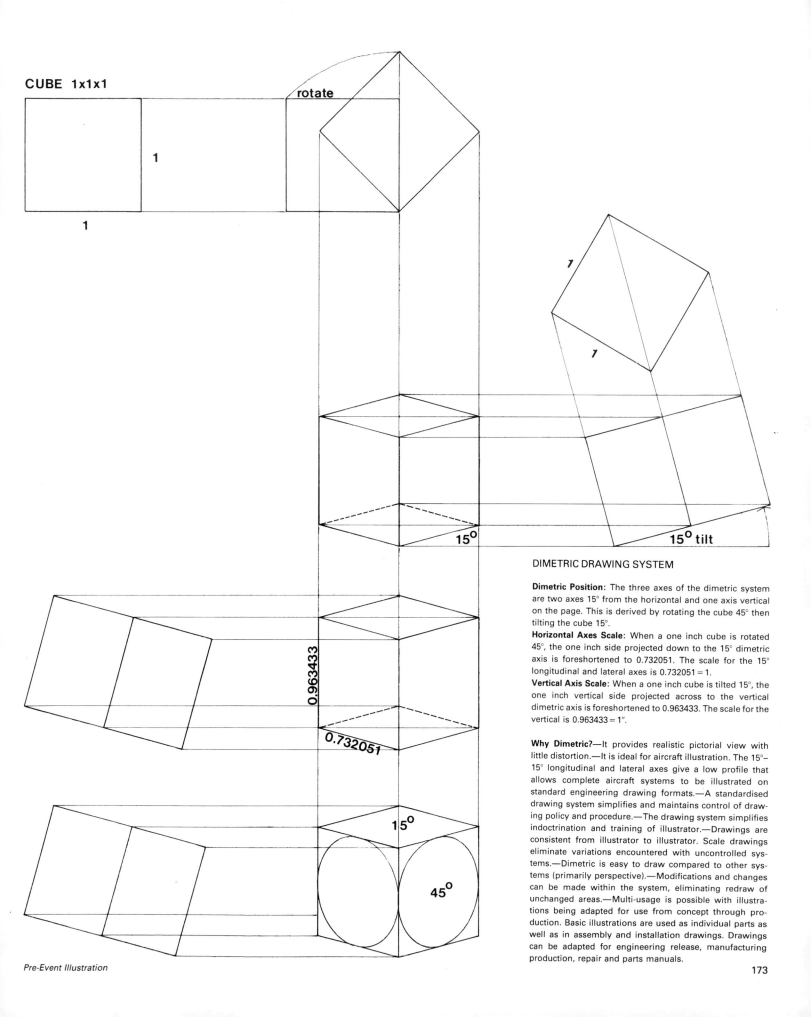

CUBE 1x1x1

1

1

1

rotate

15°

0.963433

0.732051

15° tilt

15°

15°

45°

DIMETRIC DRAWING SYSTEM

Dimetric Position: The three axes of the dimetric system are two axes 15° from the horizontal and one axis vertical on the page. This is derived by rotating the cube 45° then tilting the cube 15°.

Horizontal Axes Scale: When a one inch cube is rotated 45°, the one inch side projected down to the 15° dimetric axis is foreshortened to 0.732051. The scale for the 15° longitudinal and lateral axes is 0.732051 = 1.

Vertical Axis Scale: When a one inch cube is tilted 15°, the one inch vertical side projected across to the vertical dimetric axis is foreshortened to 0.963433. The scale for the vertical is 0.963433 = 1".

Why Dimetric?—It provides realistic pictorial view with little distortion.—It is ideal for aircraft illustration. The 15°-15° longitudinal and lateral axes give a low profile that allows complete aircraft systems to be illustrated on standard engineering drawing formats.—A standardised drawing system simplifies and maintains control of drawing policy and procedure.—The drawing system simplifies indoctrination and training of illustrator.—Drawings are consistent from illustrator to illustrator. Scale drawings eliminate variations encountered with uncontrolled systems.—Dimetric is easy to draw compared to other systems (primarily perspective).—Modifications and changes can be made within the system, eliminating redraw of unchanged areas.—Multi-usage is possible with illustrations being adapted for use from concept through production. Basic illustrations are used as individual parts as well as in assembly and installation drawings. Drawings can be adapted for engineering release, manufacturing production, repair and parts manuals.

BILL BOARD ART

LA Billboards

ACKNOWLEDGMENTS

The Guest Editor would like to thank Andreas Papadakis, publisher of Architectural Design, for his generous encouragement of this ambitious visual study of Los Angeles. He is also grateful to all Faculty members of the USC School of Architecture for their help during the research period for this transcript, and in particular to the authors of the various sub-sections, the LA Editorial Committee and the following individuals, who provided research assistance in the preparation of the general sections: David Brindle; Alson Clark; Frank Dimster; Stefanos Polyzoides; Emmet Wemple; the administrative staff of the Faculty, particularly Virginia Bissinger, Doris Rolfe and Margaret Walcutt; Tridib Banerjee and Melvin C Branch at the USC Planning School; Dr Robert Knutson of the USC Doheny Library; Leonard R Wines and John Reynolds of USC University Relations.

PHOTOGRAPHERS

John Nicolais: 2, 6, 11, 14, 26, 28, 29, 30, 31, 32, 33, 37, 38, 39, 43, 44, 45, 48, 49, 51, 54, 57, 58, 65, 68, 69, 70, 76, 77, 84, 90, 97, 108, 111, 121, 124, 125, 129, 130, 131, 134, 135, 136, 137, 138, 139, 143, 144, 145, 146, 147, 149, 151, 152, 154, 155, 156, 157, 158, 159, 160, 170. 171.

Jan Larrance: 7, 28, 31, 32, 33, 34, 35, 37, 38, 39, 42, 44, 45, 46, 48, 113, 122, 123, 124, 125, 126, 127, 129, 130, 131, 134, 135, 136, 137, 138, 144, 145, 147, 148, 149, 152, 153, 157, 159, 160.

Marvin Rand: 50, 52, 53, 56, 67, 64, 92.

Julius Schulman: 67, 74, 75, 78, 80, 82, 83, 84, 85, 86, 87, 90, 91, 95, 112.

Other photographs by: Glen Allison, Ernest Braun, David Brindle, Herbert Bruce Coss, Fred Dapprich, Chris Dawson, William Eccles, Richard Fish, Foster & Kleiser, Grover Gilchrist, Jason Hailey, Haveman, Charles Chrisopher Hill, Sam Hurst, Balthazar Korab, Dale Lang, Jack Laxer, Long Beach Independent Press, Los Angeles Police Department, Norman McGrath, Graeme Morland, John Mutlow, Richard Neutra, Stefanos Polyzoides, Tim Street Porter, James Reed, John Shadle, Sheedy & Long, Peter Suszynski, Wayne Thom, USC Department of Information, Derek Walker, Williams, Zimbaldi.

DRAWINGS

Peter Brandow: 54. **Charles Calvo:** 25. **Anko Chen:** 114. **Fred Dagdagan:** 52, 53, 68, 69. **Greene and Greene Library:** 55. **Charles Lee:** 77. **Graeme Morland:** 4, 12, 16, 17. **Kaz Nomura:** 85. **Richard Orne:** 110. **Michael Strogoff:** 21. **Janek Tanencki:** 12. **Panos Koulermos, Stefanos Polyzoides, Max Underwood:** 59, 60, 61. **Stefanos Polyzoides, Roger Sherwood, James Tice:** 82. **James Tice:** 63. **Derek Walker Associates:** 3, 14, 15, 27, 81, 146, 148, 173. **Atlas of California:** 2, 15, 18. **City of Los Angeles Planning Department:** 25. **The Southern California Association of Governments:** 36.

INSTITUTIONS

Atlas of California; California Information Almanac Company: Californian Historical Society Insurance and Trust; Data Support Unit Department of City Planning—City of LA; The Doheny Memorial Library—USC; Environmental Systems Research Institute of Redwood City; First Federal Savings and Loan of Hollywood; Foster & Kleiser; Huntington Hartford Museum Library; League of Women Voters of LA; Long Beach Independent Press; Los Angeles City Department City Planning; Los Angeles Police Department; Los Angeles Public Library; Metropolitan Water District; The Port of Long Beach Authority; The Port of Los Angeles Authority; The Southern Californian Association of Governments; University of California LA, Geography Department; The US Department of Labour and Employment; VTN Consolidated—Irving; The Western Economic Research Corporation.

INDIVIDUALS

Margaret Bach, Noel Diaz, Bob Girsch, Calvin Hamilton, Frank Hodgkiss, Eric Johnson, Judy Kosban, Anthony Lumsden, Gene MacKnight, Esther McCoy, Tom McGrath, Cesar Pelli, David Reddick, Elaine Sewell-Jones, Bruce Torrence, Dr Bill Wadsworth, Phil Watson, Willie Wilson, Gene Wolfe.

SOURCES FOR PHOTOGRAPHS IN THE LA METROPOLITAN AREA

Academy of Motion Picture Arts & Sciences, 9038 Melrose Avenue, Los Angeles, California 90069. 278–8990. Mildred Simpson, Head Librarian. A collection of several hundred thousand stills selectively chosen from films made between 1910 and 1950.

American Film Institute—Center for Advanced Film Studies, Charles Feldman Library, 501 Doheny Road, Beverly Hills, California 90210. 278–8777 ext 314. Anne Schlosser, Librarian. The Library has an extensive collection of Columbia Pictures stills from the period 1935 to the mid-1950s.

California Institute of Technology, Milikan Memorial Library—Archives, Pasadena, California 91109. 795–6811. Dr Judith R Goodstein, Institute Archivist. This collection includes b/w originals and copies as well as postcards, greeting cards, daguerreotypes, lantern slides and architectural drawings, covering the period from 1890 to the present.

Walt Disney Productions Library, 500 South Buena Vista, Burbank, California 91505. 345–3141 ext 2326 Harley Fortier, Librarian; David Smith, Archivist. Picture collection includes stills, and any kind of picture source—magazines, books, newspapers etc. Indexed in notebook form by subject, this is a young collection but growing. It began about 1960. Disney at present has one of the largest research staffs in the industry, and the collection is especially good for Western US, nature subjects and Americana.

First Federal Savings and Loan of Hollywood, 6801 Hollywood Blvd, Los Angeles, California 90028. 463–4141. Bruce Torrence, Archivist. This is a collection of historical photographs exclusively on the Hollywood area. The collection covers 1873 to the 1970s with the greatest concentration from about 1910 to the 1920s. There are about 4,000 items—negatives and prints.

Henry E Huntington Library, 1151 Oxford Road, San Marino, California 91108. 792 6141. Gary Kurutz, Photographs; Virginia Renner, Head of Reference. One of the largest historical collections in the Southern California area.

Los Angeles County Museum of Natural History, 900 Exposition Blvd, Los Angeles, California 90007. 746 0410 ext 242. John Cahoon, Archivist. This is another of Southern California's very large photograph collections. Its major focus is on Los Angeles and Southern California.

Los Angeles Public Library, 630 West 5th Street, Los Angeles, California 90017. 626 7461.

Los Angeles Times Editorial Library, Times Mirror Square, Los Angeles, California 90053. 625 2345. Mr Rosen, News Bureau.

Metro-Goldwyn-Mayer Research Library, 10202 West Washington Blvd, Culver City, California 92030. 870 3311. James J Earie, Director of Research. The Library's Picture Collection contains mainly photographs, but also includes illustrations from book and magazine sources. It is undoubtedly the largest of all the studio research collections with an estimated 250,000 items.

Northrop Institute of Technology Alumni, Aviation History Collection, 1155 West Arbor Vitae, Inglewood, California 90306. 776 5466. Professor David D Hatfield, Research Professor of Aviation History.

Security Pacific National Bank, 312 West 5th Street, Room 306, Los Angeles, California 90054. 613 6843. Victor Plukas, Bank Historian. The collection has extremely good coverage of smaller communities in Southern California, from about 1853 to the 1940s.

Title Insurance & Trust Co, Historical Photographs Collection, 433 South Spring Street, Los Angeles. California 90013. 626 2411 ext 2777 Dolores Nariman, In Charge.

Universal City Studios Research Library, 100 Universal City Plaza, Universal City, California 91608. 985 4321 ext 2493 R A Lee, Director of Research.

University of California, Los Angeles, 405 Hilgard Avenue, Los Angeles, California 90024. *Research Library, Special Collections—Photographs*, Hilda Bohem, Librarian in Charge. 825 4988. This collection has been estimated at over 300,000 items. *Theatre Arts Reading Room—Stills*. Audree Malkin, Theatre Arts Librarian. 825 4880. *Geography Department—Aerial Photographs*, Prof A R Orme, Department Head, 825 1071. This department owns two important aerial photograph collections. The Spence Collection contains oblique b/w photographs of the Los Angeles area from the 1920s. The Fairchild Collection was given to the Department after Lytton Industries took over the Fairchild Air Service.

WED Enterprises Inc, 1401 Flower Street, Glendale, California 91201. 245 8951. Jean Kenny, Librarian. WED Enterprises is the technical and engineering arm of Walt Disney Productions. They work with the designers and engineers principally for Disneyland and Disney World, and they produced attractions for the 1964 World Fair in New York.